The
Unstoppable
Writing
Teacher

M. COLLEEN CRUZ

The Unstoppable Writing Teacher

Real Strategies for the Real Classroom

FOREWORD BY
Lucy Calkins

HEINEMANN
Portsmouth, NH

Heinemann
361 Hanover Street
Portsmouth, NH 03801–3912
www.heinemann.com

Offices and agents throughout the world

The author and publisher wish to thank those who have generously given permission to reprint borrowed material:

Figure 9-3: "Spiral Model for Grammar Instruction" from *The Power of Grammar: Unconventional Approaches to the Conventions of Language* by Mary Ehrenworth and Vicki Vinton. Copyright © 2005 by Mary Ehrenworth and Vicki Vinton. Published by Heinemann, Portsmouth, NH. All rights reserved.

Cataloging-in-Publication Data is on file at the Library of Congress.
ISBN: 978-0-325-06248-8

Acquisitions Editor: Margaret LaRaia
Production Editor: Patty Adams
Cover and Interior Designs: Suzanne Heiser
Interior Illustrator: Caroline Sykora
Typesetter: Eric Rosenbloom, Kirby Mountain Composition
Manufacturing: Steve Bernier

Printed in the United States of America on acid-free paper
19 18 17 16 15   EBM   3 4 5

For Nico, the one who reminds me that, even when times are tough, there's no reason not to boogie.

Note to the Reader

There are more challenges to teaching writing than can be addressed in one book, and there are more answers, too. Let's continue the dialogue online, where we can all share ideas and learn from one another.

What makes you unstoppable or what's stopping you?

Join the conversation on Twitter, hashtag: **#unstoppablewritingteacher**

You'll find frequently asked questions addressed in depth on my blog at www.colleencruz.com/blog.htm. And, if you have questions you want answered, send them my way, via the blog or Twitter.

I hope to hear from you.

Contents

Foreword
by Lucy Calkins

As a profession, we are gripped by fear.

Think of what that has done to our teaching. Think of a time in your life—in or out of the classroom—when you were afraid of being caught, sure you would be trotted into the public square and humiliated. Go back to that moment, live in it. Feel your body clench up, feel your voice become tight. Now try to talk about your teaching.

Do you feel what fear does to you? It is a cage that traps us, alone, into our worst selves. Into a space with demons only we can see. We become the person we dread being. And, for many people, what happens is that fear causes us to retreat. We back away into our individual offices or classrooms, thinking, "I won't tell anyone about what's going wrong. I won't talk about it. I'll just pretend it doesn't exist."

The sad truth is that these times in education are such that literally thousands and thousands of teachers are living and teaching in fear, and that is not only driving people from the profession, it is driving us away from our selves. And, of course, if we want to get better as a profession and as individuals, we have to be willing to face those fears and talk about them because only by bringing them to light and problem-solving together will we grow.

Enter Colleen, that good, funny, quirky, friend/shrink/coach who says, "This is not your deep dark secret; this is part of being a teacher." Colleen goes straight into the hard parts of teaching writing—the parts that most people don't talk about, the parts that become dark secrets — and tells the truth. Like Max in Maurice Sendak's *Where the Wild Things Are*, she tames the wild things by looking into their eyes and calling them out of hiding. "I know you," she says, and calls them by name:

"I have no time for writing."

"The kids write better than I do anyway."

"I feel like a fraud."

"I think they are getting worse not better."

"I don't know how to help them."

"I don't know how to teach grammar."

"I feel so alone in this teaching."

Naming our fears isn't about confessing guilt. When we linger a bit longer in the details of our uncertainty and doubt, we can see the opportunities that lie hidden beneath. Colleen gives specific, clarifying language to help you understand what's stopping you from adding new skills and strategies to your writing teacher toolbox and then offers you loads of new ideas to experiment with. What she doesn't do is pretend that teaching is easier than it is. Reading this book will feel like a liberation. Colleen is that rare find: someone who has the wit, warmth, and experience to say that teaching writing is hard work, that no one writing teacher carries all the brilliance of the profession. While this book offers plenty of wise, practical solutions to the challenges of teaching writing, it's more than an encyclopedia of strategies, it's an invitation to embrace struggle as a way of being.

As you read Colleen describing her failures, laughing at herself, and moving forward, you'll find yourself prepared to do the same. For teachers who are willing to acknowledge the hard parts of teaching writing, this book will coach you through them. For teachers who feel that the teaching of writing is going splendidly, Colleen interrupts the artifice of sustained upbeat certainty: "Really? Everything about your writing instruction is fine?" Difficulty, she points out, is inevitable. No one ever has "enough" — be that knowledge about how to give the most helpful feedback or a large-enough library of classroom mentor texts. For all teachers, this book will offer the chance to grow and get better as a teacher of writing — not perfect — but better than you are now and hoping to improve.

Writing is struggle. If we want our students to become strong writers, then they have to become brave ones. We have to model that bravery in how we teach writing by naming the monsters that challenge us and facing them.

Once you finish this book, you'll be well prepared. You'll know more about the teaching of writing. You'll be braver.

Acknowledgments

I am grateful to all of the students and teachers who have opened their classrooms and their hearts to me over the years as I experimented with and revised the material in this book. I am most thankful to my first real home as a teacher, the place where I learned more about teaching and learning than I could ever fit in any book—P.S. 321 in Brooklyn, led by the inimitable Liz Philips. The colleagues I worked with and learned from there are among the finest educators in the world. I am also thankful for the many incredibly generous schools I have worked with in my current capacity as a staff developer. In particular I would like to thank Melanie Woods and Rebecca Fagin and their amazing team of teachers at P.S. 29. I would also like to thank Darlene Cameron and the teachers at P.S. 63, where a lot of the initial work around engagement and pop culture was piloted. Additionally, Jane Hsu and her crew of incredible teachers at P.S. 116. Rounding out the New York City school list, I'd like to thank P.S. 18, P.S. 176, P.S. 503, P.S. 199, and P.S. 59 for their generosity and time spent piloting some early versions of this work. I am also thankful to one of my earliest and longest-standing incubators, a school I almost always try out my newest thinking on: Hope Street School in Huntington Park, California, led by the fearless Pam Lemieux. And, I would like to thank the inspiring teachers at Hewlett Elementary School in New York for being some of my biggest cheerleaders as I slogged forward, as well as John Strohschein, Sharon Chung, and Kara Arnold for sharing their students' work.

I am deeply thankful for the generosity of one of my biggest mentors, Lucy Calkins. In the earliest stages of developing this book, when it was just a tickle of an idea, Lucy took the time to sit on the floor and confer with me about what I was trying to do. She has been a die-hard supporter of both this book and my work for many years.

Additionally, I am profoundly grateful for the support of her organization, the Teachers College Reading & Writing Project. I have been a member of it for over a decade and I am constantly awed by the knowledge and kindness my colleagues past and present have shared with me. The senior leaders of the organization, Laurie Pessah, Kathleen Tolan, Mary Ehrenworth, and Amanda Hartman have been enthusiastic and patient as I took time to work out the kinks in this book. I am especially grateful to Brooke Gellar for reminding me to look on the bright side; "It could be worse" is my new favorite optimistic-pessimistic saying. I am also thankful to Carla España for early reads of the manuscript. Jennifer Serravallo was instrumental in kicking my butt into gear when I needed it most. Cheryl Tyler, Tim Lopez, Beth Neville, Shana Frazin, Cory Gillette, and Julia Mooney have also been important players. This book, especially the chapter on English Language Learners, is a million times stronger because Emily De Liddo went over it with a fine-tooth comb. I am very thankful for her wisdom and insights. I would also like to thank Carl Anderson, who more than a decade ago planted the idea in my head that I should write a book, which resulted in *Independent Writing*. He has been a constant book-pusher ever since, and I am most grateful for the consistent nudging, advice, and commiseration.

I would also like to give a special thank-you to my dear friend and colleague Kate Roberts, who was a friend before she was a colleague but has now become such a mash-up of both it is hard to know which end is up. Maggie Beattie Roberts has also played an important role in that mash-up, and I cannot remember where the friendship ends and the colleague begins with her either.

This book has been through many iterations over the years. It was originally slated to be an entire book about using pop culture in the writing workshop. My editor, Margaret LaRaia, patiently worked with me through that process, all the way up to the contract where I balked, and started over again, this time with the concept of the book you are holding in your hand. I have never worked with an editor as closely as I have worked with Margaret. Yet somehow, through encouragement, YouTube links, book recommendations, and a few choice curse words, she managed to midwife me through some of the more difficult aspects of the book and mostly hide her apprehensions until after the fact. I am very thankful to have had her.

I am also grateful to the entire team at Heinemann, but especially my first Heinemann editor, Kate Montgomery, whose continued support in my work still carries me forward. I'd also like to thank Suzanne Heiser for the fantastic design, Patty Adams for the inspired production, Sarah Fournier for keeping everything from crashing, Brett Whitmarsh for social media support, and Kim Cahill for being an all-around marketing rock star.

I'd like to thank my Wednesday Night writing group: Kristin Beers, Australia Fernandez, Kerri Hook, Connie Pertuz-Meza, Barbara Pinto, and Sarah Scheldt. I would also like to thank Caroline Sykora for her amazing illustrations.

My family and friends have been ridiculously supportive during this entire process. I have been basically missing for the past five years either having children or writing books. I owe them some time and so much more. I would like to thank especially my parents, Joan and Wil Cruz, for leaving me be and not asking too many questions; my editor/writer brother Mike Cruz for being the most empathetic cheerleader a sister could ask for; Marge and Collette Baldasare for letting me disappear all the time without a word of complaint. I would also like to thank my older son Sam for dragging me out of my office with a firm, "Work is closed, Mommy." And I am honored by the joy Nico gives me, even though I've been working on this book for his entire life so far.

Lastly, I would like to thank, celebrate, and admire my partner Nadine Baldasare. Her tireless support of this book, thankless picking-up of my dropped balls, and countless days and nights of taking over parenting duties while I holed up in my writing hovel, all while managing to create her own inspiring art, was something to behold.

Introduction

"I Am a Pessimist"

I am a pessimist.

   I'll get back to that. First, pop quiz — how do these things fit together? What is their relationship?

Take a minute to jot in the margin how you think those three things could go together. By the end of this book, I assure you, if you have not already deciphered the answer, you will figure it out then.

I want to thank you for taking the time to read this book. I know how busy you are and I know that taking time to read professional literature means you are not doing something else: grading, planning, meeting with a parent, tutoring a kid, drinking wine with friends, sleeping . . . Instead, you are doing something for your own professional development, and that is hugely admirable. Before you embark on this book I'd like to suggest that you reflect a bit on the lens you plan to use while reading it.

All of us experience things in life through lenses. Sometimes we watch television with the lens of accuracy. We listen to our administrators with the lens of practicality. Perhaps you're the type of person that looks at everything in life through the lens of equity.

I, of course, as a pessimist, do almost everything, including reading professional literature and writing it, through the lens of trouble. My ears sort of perk up like the old RCA dog. I choose books based on the fact that they are about trouble, or are about dealing with trouble. I struggle with books and other kinds of professional development that seem too positive. Of course, not everything needs to be based on trouble, but whenever an author starts to focus on it (tricky conferences, curriculum development, accommodations), I sit up and take note.

So, yes, I really am a pessimist. And I believe some of you are already considering putting this book down.

But, the thing is, I'm a rather positive pessimist. I have come to believe being a pessimist is mostly a good thing. I was raised a pessimist. You know how the people who take care of you when you're little often sing little ditties as they wash the dishes or take you to school or mow the lawn? My mother's two favorite songs to sing while tooling around were Ray Charles's "I'm Busted" and the Everly Brothers' "Problems." Remember that song? In case you don't, it's worth a listen. The song talks about how the singer's life is falling apart—in love, in school, even with his dog. This is a song my mom hummed or sang every day.

My family has always embraced struggle. We give big old bear hugs to adversity. Things have never been easy for anyone in my family and we have evolved to sort of embrace that. To revel in the trouble. Not mope. Revel.

Not because we're masochists or martyrs, although some of us are. But because of two reasons. The first is that *hard things do consistently happen.* Maybe my whole family was born while Mercury was in retrograde. So, we might as well just embrace this reality, the same way people live right beside the 1,500 active volcanoes all over the world, knowing they can erupt at any time. But also knowing that, volcano or not, a home can be destroyed anytime. Just the chances are greater that when you live near a volcano, you can predict how it will happen. And when they erupt, as they sometimes do, you are prepared to either clean up and rebuild or decide now's the time to move.

When you're pessimistic, or at least my take on pessimism, you are sort of always expect-ing bad things to happen, or at least for good things to *not* happen. So you're never shocked or taken aback when they do happen. You lost your job? Of course you did. There was a car accident? Pass the salt. The roof caught on fire on Christmas? I'm surprised it didn't happen sooner.

The second reason I've learned to embrace the hard stuff is because every time something bad happens, it's an opportunity for something different, maybe even better to happen. When Dad lost his job, he went back to school and became a teacher — in his 60s. Since the car accident, there's a new lighted-up stop sign that flashes at the corner where Mom was hit. After the Christmas fire, the insurance paid for a roof that badly needed repairs before the fire. (These are all true stories, by the way.)

So, yes, all these bad things, all bad things that happen to my family, that happen to you, that happen to your students, are in fact terrible. And are to be experienced fully, and suffered through and felt and mourned. There is actually research that shows that being pessimistic, embracing difficulties and hardships and seeing them for what they really are (crappy), is a much healthier and, strangely, happier way of being than thinking positively and being optimistic all the time. That, in fact, sometimes thinking positively all the time is more stressful because when bad things happen, positive thinkers tend to blame themselves, and think somehow they were responsible for what happened to them.

This leaning into pessimism has mostly turned out to be a good thing for me and the people close to me. This sort of wide-awake, very aware, and very realistic way of living life makes it much less likely that we'll be caught unawares. From the sort of morbid (kiss Nana goodbye, she might not be alive much longer), which set us up to never have regretted not saying our proper goodbyes, to the more practical—like when I was a teenager, all of my friends' parents told them not to drink. But my mom was the only one who said, "Listen, at parties in high school, many of them will have alcohol. You don't want to drink. But, if you just say you don't want to drink, you will probably be bothered until you do. So, instead, what you do, when you get to the party, find one of those red cups, half fill it with beer. Take a sip so it's on your breath. Then go about your business, holding your cup. Feel free to act a little goofy, or a little loud. Everyone will think you're drinking and they'll leave you alone."

Learning how to anticipate problems, actually look for them, and then face them head on has deeply affected the way I live.

One might have guessed by my self-proclaimed pessimism that I am not a big fan of the overemphasis some people put on positive thinking. You would be correct. But I do know that positive thinking works for many people. In fact, most of my dearest friends and colleagues cringe every time I go on about how it's better to expect problems and be prepared for them than to be surprised about them. I have lots of respect for people who are optimistic. For a long time I wished I could be that way myself.

That said, I do have some rather strong feelings about the pressure people in general, teachers in specific, have to be positive all the time. Whether I am skimming social media or simply looking at the latest list of best-selling self-help books, there is an overabundance of belief in the fact that positive thinking is not just a powerful choice for people dealing with struggle, but the *only* way to go. One particularly powerful self-help tome goes as far as to say that if one dares to *even think* negative thoughts, one is attracting negative energy and is to blame for whatever might befall.

One of the huge downsides to this sort of positive thinking is that more people than I can count have felt guilty when faced with struggles and challenges. They have shared their obstacles and then immediately followed up with, "But I shouldn't complain. I am fortunate in a lot of ways." Let me be clear—I have no use for complaining followed by inaction. There are few things that annoy me more than people sitting around a table talking about all the terrible things happening, but then not making any plans to do anything about it. While I do believe that complaining, and only complaining, is no way to live a life, I also believe that discussing trouble can help find a path to problem solving. It's often in the discussion that possible solutions come to light. I have come to think a few things about the obstacles that get in the way of teachers:

1. The classroom is a challenging place to be.

2. By expecting and looking for trouble we are more likely to be prepared.

3. With very few exceptions, most difficulties we face in the classroom can be made less difficult, if not vanquished entirely.

When we teach and live expecting, looking for, and preparing for trouble (hopefully many of you live in this way), we cease to be simply passive observers. We aren't just only looking at the pretty things, ignoring that bad things happen, or simply complaining about them until someone else comes along and fixes them (or doesn't), just along for the ride in our own lives. We are taking the wheel. We aren't sightseeing, we are *driving*.

I was sharing this little piece of who I am, my practical pessimistic worldview, with Barb Silverario, a literacy coach at Canton Intermediate School in Connecticut. And she looked at me and nodded, completely knowingly. "You'd get along well with my husband," she said, laughing. Her husband is a career Army officer who has done several tours of duty in Iraq and Afghanistan and is currently on active duty in DC. "When I complain about something, Dave always says, 'You've got to tighten those bootlaces and march toward the battlefield.'"

That phrase just took my breath away. So much stronger, so much more active than what I had even been thinking about and talking about. But so true to the core of what I believe.

Tighten those laces and march toward the battlefield.

Meet it head on, that is exactly what firefighters, doctors, and teachers do too — every day.

That position, that soldier's philosophy of when there's trouble, not running away, or covering our eyes or waiting for someone else to come along, but rather, to get our selves set and head directly to it, I realized in a minute that it was the philosophy I had been raised in, but perhaps not spoken as concisely as Barb's husband said it.

Let me be clear. I am not at all suggesting that teachers are in fact soldiers. I know that there are very strong opinions on both sides of the fence and everywhere in between about soldiers and the military in particular. But, I do believe that teachers and soldiers and firefighters and doctors and anyone else with an occupation that requires trouble in order to fill it, have something in common. All of us in these sorts of professions go against what most typical people would do when they see trouble — avoid it. Instead, we grab our gear and run *toward* it. When Barb told me about her husband's slogan, "Tighten those laces and head toward the battlefield," I envisioned that teacher looking over her class list right before the school year starts and smiling because she is already imagining all the challenges her students will bring to her and how she can't wait to face them head on. I thought of a colleague who walked into the principal's office to thank the principal for placing a particularly high-needs kid in his class because he knew he could help the student. The list goes on and on.

I recently spoke to Owen, a trouble-chaser if there ever was one. Owen is both a fourth-grade teacher and volunteer firefighter in East Hampton, New York, and I wondered a bit about what he thought of facing trouble. I told him about how I see such a connection between people in risk-centric occupations and teachers, and how they are seemingly out of their minds in similar ways. He laughed. "I mean, how do you just rush headlong into a fire?" I asked. "Do they train you how to do it? Because I feel like human instinct when you see fire is to run the other way."

He laughed again. "They don't have to train us to run into a fire," he said. "You're either just the kind of person who wants to run into a fire or you're not." I had a hard time picturing this fourth-grade teacher whose class I had visited, whose student writing I had read tons of times before, with his firefighter's gear on. But I had immense respect for it.

"But aren't you scared?" I asked. "Don't you have to overcome a desire to run away?"

"No. I like running to the fire. When I climb on a roof and cut a hole in that roof so that the fire gets air and whooshes up — I know when that hole is cut that the fire is almost over. That I just saved lives. I live for that."

I've also come to believe, now more than ever, that when we signed up for teaching, we were signing up for a kind of battlefield, a kind of firefighting, a kind of lifesaving.

So, how do we do this thing? How do we decide to embrace a pessimistic nature, face problems head on, tighten up those laces and march toward the battlefield?

In this book, I am proposing one possible protocol for embracing problems. It's by far not the only protocol for problem solving that there is. You might even have heard of or created better. But this one is definitely tailored to the educator population, particularly the ones who expect trouble, see it as something that can and should be addressed, and want to develop a repertoire of strategies for dealing with it:

- Choose a problem to focus on. And celebrate the opportunity it offers.

- Study why it stops us and how it can be an opportunity.

- Experiment — try something.

- Plan for ongoing work.

- **Choose a problem to focus on. And celebrate the opportunity it offers.** Of course, I realize that I assumed you had problems. But, on the off chance that there are currently no problems or struggles going on in your classroom, no obstacles that are trying to stop you from being the kind of teacher you want to be, know that it is highly likely you will come across a struggle some-day. And then this step will become helpful for you. For the rest of us, it's not so much finding problems, as deciding which one to address first.

  My advice: you don't have to start with your biggest problems. In the first chapter of this book I will make a case for picking small, bite-sized problems first. And then working your way up from there. Just know that the most important thing is to pick a problem you feel needs to be handled, but is not so overburdensome that you will feel discouraged. You'll get to those. You just probably don't want to start there.

  This book will go over some of the more common concerns and struggles I have heard about or been asked to weigh in on over my years as an educator. These include:

- Working with sophisticated, sometimes intimidatingly so, writers

- Helping students who have big learning challenges

- Teaching students who are learning to speak English alongside writing

- Struggling to find resources

- Finding time to teach writing in an overpacked schedule

- Building agency in students who are overly dependent on us

- Successfully teaching grammar

- Dealing with professional loneliness

- Communicating with adults who do not understand writing workshop

- Combating boredom with student topics

- Searching for ways to connect with kids whose pop culture interests can seem far removed from the classroom

While I worked hard to get as much input as possible from as many educators as possible, it's also possible that some of you might not see the problem that you would like to address first in the pages of this book. If that's the case, know that the chapter called "Name Your Monster" is written to help you design your own action plans for any struggles you might still be grappling with. Additionally, I suggest you visit my blog at colleencruz.com, which I regularly update with questions sent to me from teachers.

I'm also going to suggest that you celebrate once you find the problem you will attack first. The idea that there is room for celebrations in a pessimist's heart might surprise you. But, remember, pessimists are happy too. And, as we talked about before, trouble and problems help us to grow, and have many fringe benefits worth celebrating. We might get to know a student better who has flown below the radar. We might find ourselves having new opportunities to bond with colleagues we have worked with for years. We might find ourselves discovering that it is time to update our resumés. We might celebrate the fact that we are not letting self-doubt paralyze us and we are taking action for our kids. No matter what, problems mean that something different is going to happen. For our mental health, it seems wise to embrace that reality.

- **Study why it stops us and how it can be an opportunity.**
Make some time to study the problem closely. Look around the situation. Above it, under it. And you might want to do more than watch. Try looking a little ahead of the problem, a little after it. What are the things that caused this to be the way it is? What are the effects this struggle has on our students or our classroom?

Try to study absolutely every aspect in ways that match the problem itself. Observe. Listen. Ask. Read. Leave no stone unturned. Try to write down anything you've learned. These notes can help you stay clearheaded and not jump to any conclusions. Forcing ourselves to get a fresh look at a problem often solves many more problems than just the one we were originally focused on.

For example, in Chapter 9, when we take a look at the slippery nature of grammar instruction, we will look not only at the importance of a grammar curriculum, but also at how powerful it is when a building shares a vision that offers consistency to the students across the years.

Also, as part of the studying of the problem, you will want to consider the obstacles that will likely get in your way as well. In Gabriele Oettingen's recently published book, *Rethinking Positive Thinking*, she discusses important research about the difficulties positive thinkers have in meeting their goals. So much of what she writes about resonates with my own thinking over the past few years about problems in the classroom. Oettingen discusses how people who actually accomplish their goals are usually not positive but rather realistic (I would call them pessimistic) because they anticipate obstacles that will inevitably get in the way of their goals. They then consider how they will overcome these obstacles before even embarking on their journey. By expecting trouble and making a plan for dealing with those problems, these successful people were more likely to be prepared to face things head on, as opposed to being derailed.

Throughout this book, I recommend a similar idea. I will suggest that, as you study your struggle, what causes it, why it's difficult, and why it's an opportunity, you also consider what might get in your way. For example, in Chapter 2, when discussing ways to support sophisticated writers who can intimidate us with their skill, we will also stop to consider the difficulty that comes from writers who might push back. In Chapter 4, when we discuss teaching students who are learning English, we will pause to think of our own anxieties about language and inadequacies.

Once you have studied likely causes and effects of problems, as well as obstacles that might trip you up on the way to working through it, you will be well positioned for action.

- **Experiment — try something.**
Now you need to act. What's tricky is that so many of us educator types are perfectionist by nature. The idea of going into problem-solving mode, not being sure if what we're about to do will really work, can be a daunting thing. Maybe I should wait a little longer, do more recon? Maybe I need to enlist more help? And this can sometimes be the case.

I can speak for myself here — when I was in the classroom, I spent a lot of time wringing my hands about problems, studying them from all angles, but then hesitated when it came time for action. I felt like the solutions I came up with couldn't possibly be the right ones since I was the one who came up with them. If I could talk to my former teacher self, I would tell her, unless it's a life-or-death situation, just try something. Taking action toward solving problems goes a long way toward solving them, faster than just waiting until the magic-bullet answer comes along.

- **Plan for ongoing work.**

   After trying a strategy, take some time to reflect. Did it work? Did it sort of work? Did it not work at all? What could be done better? Differently? What did you learn in this process *so far?*

   Oftentimes the strategy works — and it's time to give yourself a well-earned pat on the back. Other times the strategy works — temporarily, and you will need to repeat it again, or adjust it as time goes by. Still other times you will realize you completely missed the mark. In those cases, try to get yourself excited about the fact that this precious trouble is going to be around to teach you some more things for a while. If that's the case, you can head back to the starting line again, fresh eyes at the ready. No matter what, after reflecting, most of us will realize that there is ongoing work to do, if not directly with the problem we were addressing, then likely with a related problem.

Throughout the problem-solving sections that make up the bulk of this book, I want to be very clear: everything I suggest in terms of problem solving comes from my own work in classrooms or the experiences and knowledge base of my incredible colleagues. But, that said, as with any book, not every strategy will work for every situation. But the good news is that you already knew that. As part of the effort to offer as many examples as possible, I have given a majority of the students and a few of the teachers described in this book pseudonyms, or they are a compilation of several people I have known, or both. I have also changed a few details when appropriate to protect privacy.

I tried to also address the fact that not every problem will be addressed, not every solution proposed will work, by including some proactive suggestions to support your ongoing work as a teacher of writing. I hope in the pages of this book you find ideas, or ideas that inspire ideas, that can help you stay happy and healthy in this crazy and awe-inspiring profession for a long time.

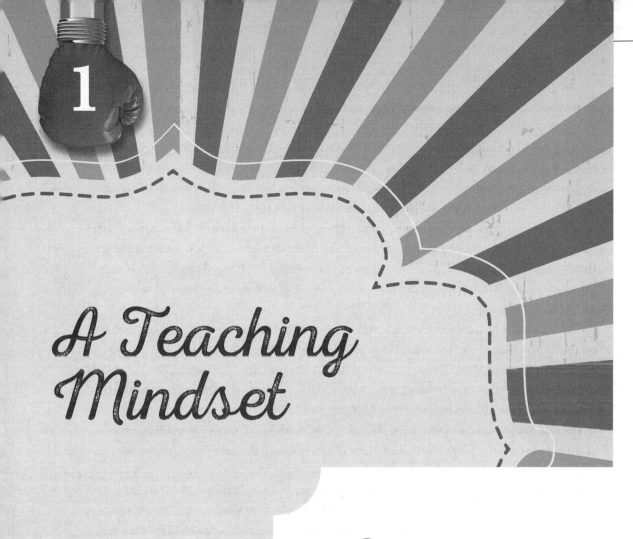

A Teaching Mindset

1

I think you might have noticed, already, that I strongly believe that teaching, and especially teaching writing, is very hard work. Sometimes, seemingly impossible work. We learn. We create. We teach. We revise. We learn more. Then the cycle repeats. However, one of the things I found most frustrating when I was in my own classroom was the way in which the things I learned one year, or perhaps even over ten years, could not simply be used over and over ad infinitum. It was exhausting thinking of how every year I had to create so much that was new.

Yet, I know that teaching children is in fact a dynamic field. It's both a scientific and artistic profession. Scientific because new research and new ideas are learned every day as we learn more and more about brains, development, and how humans learn best. It's an art because there is a fair amount of vision, creation, and heart needed in order to decide what is best for our students. Neither science nor the arts are ever stagnant. New knowledge, new inspirations, new materials change the way that scientists and artists can practice their craft.

I believe, as many people do, that teachers are both scientists and artists.

Yet, so many of us, myself included, wish time and again that once we have learned something, once we have mastered a lesson, a teaching method, a unit, a rubric, a parent letter, that it should be preserved in amber — never to be touched or changed again. This is very understandable. You work so damn hard. Why can't our work be preserved and used again and again for always?

The answer is of course: we are scientists and artists. And just as we would be horrified by the notion that a scientist today was still using radioactive materials without protective equipment the way Marie Curie did, or repelled by the notion of someone killing and stuffing an endangered animal to paint it the way Audubon did, we should feel just as horrified by the notion that a teacher in her thirtieth year would be teaching exactly the same things in the same way as she did when she started. We have all heard stories about those teachers. There are even sayings about them: "He's been teaching the same year for twenty-five years."

Lately I've been having more and more empathy for teachers who are like that, loath to change and loath to let go of tried-and-true methods. "If it ain't broke . . ." Maybe it's because I have felt that way in the past. Maybe it's because I'm getting older myself. Maybe it's because I have noticed that the amount of new information coming at educators these days, the number of new mandates and new standards and new tests, seems to keep piling on and on. It's enough to make a teacher who cares about her kids and about her profession want to dig in her heels and say, no more changes please. At least not today.

I also think I have more empathy since I've become a parent. I now have two small children. And every day they do something fantastic. I wish every day could begin with my toddler's wobbly giggling dance as he spins around the living room to the newest Dan Zanes tune. I wish every day could end with my preschooler sitting on the couch poring over a pile of picture books, me giggling and gasping. My eyes fill with tears every time we clean the boys' closet of clothes they have outgrown and will never wear again. I want to put the whole world on pause in those moments, only to rewind it and play it again.

Those little sparks of magic, sometimes big firework-sized magic, happen every day in our classrooms too. They usually come after we have cried and sweated and bled all over our classrooms. We have created the perfect unit, demonstrated the perfect piece of writing for the ideal writing strategy, held the most transformational conference with the most helpful toolkit in the world, and then we have to lay it aside and move on. Because the next class, or the next day, or the next student will most likely need something different.

Now, that's not to say that we can't bring some things forward with us as we move forward through our days and years. Part of the "work smarter not harder" ethos is that we salvage the things we can reuse as often as possible. I am a big believer in that. I am also a big believer in taking stock of things we used years before and have not looked at in a long time to see if there is some nugget, some little gem, that we could recycle and refashion into something useful again. I also believe that we learn things that are permanent, things that become part of our philosophy, part of our beings. Those too should become our lodestars. They will never waiver.

But, the actual work, well, I find it is easier to move forward and be more accepting of the changes our field brings to us, our students bring to us, if we shift the way we are looking at things.

❋ The Sand Mandala: Teaching Is About Impermanence

A little over a decade ago, the Dalai Lama came to New York. When he was here I learned about something called a sand mandala. If you're unfamiliar with the sand mandala, I encourage you to jump online and watch a video clip of one being built. Here's a clip I particularly like for its brevity and thoroughness: http://religion.blogs.cnn.com/2010/06/02/a-mandala-in-minutes/.

Full disclosure, I am not a sand mandala expert, so know that the following description is to the best of my knowledge. Sand mandalas are created by Buddhist monks. It takes years of study for a monk to learn what he needs to know about them. When sand mandalas are made, they are created by a group of monks, working together. A design is chosen and then sketched out on a table using rope and rulers. Then, using simple tools, the monks proceed to form the mandala with colorful grains of sand, placing the sand almost grain by grain onto the design. These intricate designs take several days to complete. They are brightly colored and delicate, exquisite to look at. When they complete the mandala it is then swept away. With a sort of broom. The swept sand is then gathered and dropped into a river or other body of water as a blessing.

The sand mandala is meant to be a reminder of life's impermanence. That anything made by humans is not permanent. The value of the sand mandala is in the process, the thinking, meditating, and learning as the creation is happening. The finished piece hardly matters because it was never meant to last.

This reminds me so much of teaching.

What we do as teachers is so much like creating a sand mandala on any given level. So much of our day-to-day work is done in the name of setting up our students so they can be successful and independent in that grade's work without us. We know we have done our job well when we are walking around the classroom, all of the students are deeply invested in their writing, and no one needs our help. We don't want our students to permanently need us. It is the fact that they are ours *temporarily* that gives us that sense of urgency, as well as a sense of satisfaction, when they get where we need them to be before we say goodbye.

We are also creating teacher sand mandalas whenever we do something with our materials and plans. Whether we create an amazing grading toolkit, or the perfect mentor text library, or design the most amazing personal narrative unit the world has ever seen — we know that eventually those things will need to change. Things wear out. Our learning grows. New books are published. Children's tastes change.

I find that this perspective on teaching, and on writing for that matter, has greatly altered the way I approach everything, for the better. As you know, I am a deep, confirmed pessimist. Sometimes that can be a bit of a downer to those around me, since I expect everything to go wrong all the time. However, the sand mandala has actually helped me see some things in an almost positive light. It helps me to see one more purpose to things changing, failing, moving on.

When I work on developing a new writing unit, I try to be as much as possible in the moment of the planning. I celebrate all the learning I am doing, all the new things I've discovered. Yes, I feel good when it's done. But I know that almost as soon as I have said a unit is planned, it has already begun to change. Because the students change, and the days change, even the core concepts of what I thought I was going to teach might change because the students need something different. When I write a chapter for a new book, such as this one, I know, I actually expect, that just as many chapters will be greatly altered or thrown away as will stay completely intact. It's not the chapter that matters, it's the process of writing it.

I encourage you to consider, just for this moment, your teaching as crafting a sand mandala. You go through your year, a year that took many years and months to prepare for. You create something beautiful and intricate and exquisite to admire. Then, you sweep it away. You drop it into the river of teaching time as a blessing for your future teaching self, for other teachers, and more importantly, all the children who have not yet been taught.

✳ Go for the Calf

Perhaps you decided that you are going to embrace the idea of teaching as a sand mandala. Perhaps you already thought of it that way, or something like that. But you're still wondering how to go about getting started with the problem-solving aspects of it.

The story of Milo of Croton, an ancient Greek athlete and friend of Pythagoras, goes that he was the strongest and best wrestler in Greece. He had won every athletic contest possible, including six Olympic titles. But the thing that impressed people the most about him was his strength. He was widely known as the strongest man in Greece. He was known to carry a full-grown bull on his shoulders. Which, because at first it seems an impossible feat, most certainly must be a myth.

Until you hear how the story says he did it — by starting with a small newborn calf, which he carried with him everywhere. He fed the calf and cared for the calf. And carried the calf across his shoulders everywhere he went. As the calf grew, Milo's strength grew along with it. The calf eventually became a full-grown bull and Milo's strength was now at its apex.

He could pick up any bull he saw if he wanted to — something he might not have been able to do if that was where he started. Of course, once Milo had developed his strength in this way, he did what anyone else would do — he slaughtered and ate the bull.

My point is not that you should slaughter and eat a bull, but rather, that to get started on tackling problems you will face, or are perhaps currently facing, you will want to go in with your eyes wide open, pessimism firmly at the ready, expecting there to be problems. But, perhaps more importantly still, don't go try to grab the bull first. Go for the calf—a small problem that you can grow your muscles with, knowing that, of course, all problems are relative. And knowing that by making your problem-solving muscles bigger gradually, you will be able to handle the bull (in every sense of the word) easily, soon enough.

But how does one make one's problem-solving muscles stronger?

✳ Work Smarter, Not Harder

A very long time ago, very early in my career, I remember once laboring until almost 9:00 at night in my classroom. Not unusual for me. I don't remember what I was working on. I just know I was sitting on the floor with my shoes off and the radio blasting. I was trying to just finish whatever I was working on when a colleague who was leaving for the night stopped by my room. She told me I needed to go home. "I will, I will. I just need to finish this," I said.

She smiled at me, but stood in the doorway a little longer. Like there was something she wanted to say. "What?" I said. "You think I'm crazy?"

"Nope," she said. "I just think you need to work smarter, not harder." I heard her steps echo down the empty hallway, my eyes blurry with exhaustion. In my memory she was whistling. But that moment was absolutely a pivot point for me. I realized that so much of what I had been doing as a teacher was working very hard and not getting very far. I would create lots and lots of stuff, plan for hours, and yet, I could rarely trace back the impact of all my hard work on my students. I started to think that in my desire to become a good teacher for my students I was in fact taking time off my career. I was exhausting myself.

I realized all at once that I was covering for my anxieties and lack of know-how by working as hard as I possibly could, so at the very least I could say I had done the best I possibly could. But I knew, now, that it wasn't the best I could do. That the best I could do would require putting down the tools and thinking a bit. I would need to do less of the heavy lifting myself. I needed my colleagues for support and collaboration. I needed to hand more of the work of learning to my students. In order to get control and actually improve the situation that was my teaching, I needed to let some of that control go.

I am now a big believer in working smarter, not harder. Before I roll up my sleeves and get to work on a problem—almost any problem—I stop and think for a bit about the best possible approach to solving the problem. Can I call a friend for advice? Can I ask for a volunteer to share the load? Can I teach the students how to handle this? How might technology help?

While it has likely always been true about teachers (Plato probably worked way too hard lesson planning for Aristotle and his classmates), lately I have begun to believe that teachers seem to be working harder than ever. There are dozens of reasons for this: rising levels of child poverty, new teacher evaluation systems, district learning targets that are constantly moving — all in an information age in which content and skill knowledge grow exponentially by the minute. We don't need to add our own selves and our hard-work addiction habits to the mix.

As you move through your day, your week, your month, I encourage you to take small pauses before you act. Ask yourself — is there a way to work smarter and not harder here? Before you pass out those papers. Before you hand-write every rubric. Before you create another assessment when you could simply read through your students' notebooks. Because, the truth is, even if you endeavored to work smarter every single time you lifted a finger to work, you would still be working hard. And while working hard might make us feel a little better in the short run, in the long run, we need our energy in order to face the other problems yet to come.

✸ You Can't Fix Every Problem, But You Can Respond

Teachers, as first responders, often see things that we would rather not see. Every day, teachers face endless problems from administration, curriculum, and students. There is no way that we can expect teachers to fix every problem that comes your way. This is not just because there are so many of them, although that's true. It is also because some problems are not in our purview.

You have a student who comes to school hungrier on Monday morning because, as you happen to know, she only eats when school is in session. You have to administer a standardized test to severely disabled students who have made remarkable progress — over two years' growth — but are still two years behind your grade's standards, knowing that they will feel demoralized by the process. You have an administrator who has a completely different philosophy about learning and teaching than you do.

These are all problems that most of us will not be able to solve. These are the kinds of problems that can make us lose sleep at night. But, I would argue, we can return to the image of the sand mandala when facing them. Beauty is not permanent and neither is the hard stuff. Things change. They always do. So, in the absence of being able to introduce a permanent solution, we can still engage in the process of problem solving. We can stock our classroom cupboard with granola bars. We can let that student know we will help them learn and grow so much this year. We can be transparent with our students about the standardized tests. Explain what it means to have a standardized test for children who are not standardized. We can show them ways to make the most of the experience, all the while pointing out the real, true measures of what they have learned. We can gather close to other colleagues who share a similar educational philosophy and feed each other's souls as we build a learning and teaching community within a larger context.

No, we can't solve all the problems we will be faced with. But we can choose how to respond to them. And our responses and the way we let the responses affect us will make all the difference.

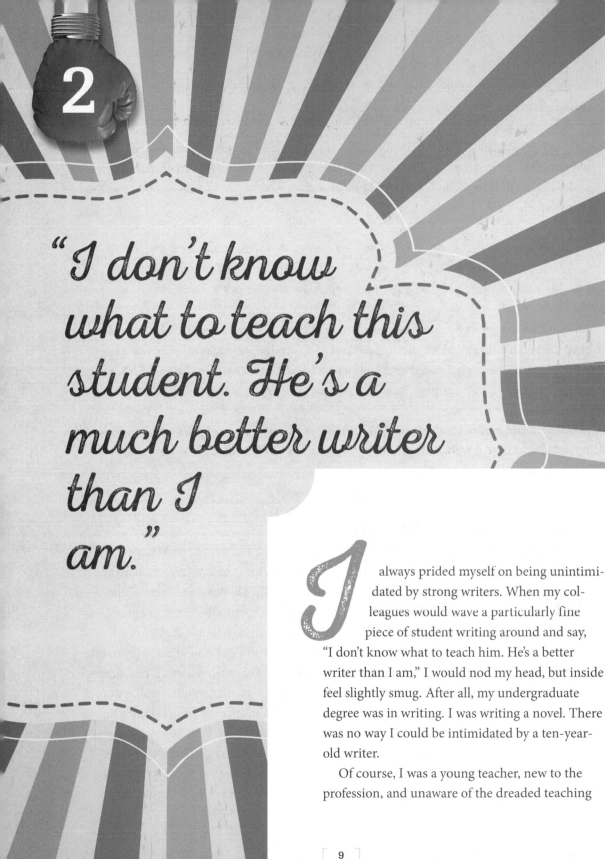

2

"I don't know what to teach this student. He's a much better writer than I am."

I always prided myself on being unintimidated by strong writers. When my colleagues would wave a particularly fine piece of student writing around and say, "I don't know what to teach him. He's a better writer than I am," I would nod my head, but inside feel slightly smug. After all, my undergraduate degree was in writing. I was writing a novel. There was no way I could be intimidated by a ten-year-old writer.

Of course, I was a young teacher, new to the profession, and unaware of the dreaded teaching curse that whatever you feel smug about, whatever you are *sure* you can handle, the teaching gods will make sure to knock you down a peg.

Enter Hannah.

Hannah's mother was an excellent teacher. Her father was a creative professional. She walked into my fourth-grade classroom able to write two or three well-structured, strongly crafted pages in thirty minutes. I would pull up a chair next to her and she would be writing something like this:

> *Angeline felt as though the devil started controlling the neighborhood children and made them not want to play with her during this beautiful weather. She felt as though a gate separated her from happiness and led her to boredom . . .*

My excellent conferring move was to smile, compliment her, and then say, "Can't wait to read it when it's done!" before running as fast I could to the next student—the one I knew what to teach. The more I pored over Hannah's writing, the more overwhelmed I felt. Everything I taught I saw on her page. Complex structures, sophisticated word choice, figurative language. Gulp.

All at once I realized that no one was immune to running into a child, or in some cases, a class full of children, who are motivated writers with a strong skill set who leave you at a loss.

✳ What Stops Us: The Stakes Are High

Even though at first glance, most outsiders, who either aren't teachers or don't have these students in their classrooms, have a hard time imagining what could possibly be hard about teaching students who have strong writing skills ("Oh, I wish I had your problems," they say). We know that in fact, these students can be among the toughest we've ever taught.

First of all, one of the ways these highly skilled writers can be tough is that we don't always know what to teach them. We have used up all our strategies and ideas in the main instruction of a unit, and they can already do all of our extra-special, tricks-up-our-sleeves tips. When we go to teach them, whether when thinking about minilessons, small group, or conferences, we are often at a loss for what we can teach them that they don't already know.

Another way they can be tough is that we can forget about them. Whole weeks can go by and since they don't ask for help, and we don't see anything sending up flares from their notebooks, we can speed by their seats without pausing, believing that not only are they fine, but they are doing better than most of their peers. We are not always right about this.

And, with some strong writers, it is challenging to teach them because they push back. They have been told their whole lives that they are great writers. It's entirely probable that you are not the first teacher who was intimidated or impressed by them. It is likely that many adults gave them a lot of effusive praise, but not a lot of critical feedback. Because of this, when they are approached with the notion that there might be something for them to learn, something for them to improve upon, they often balk. "It's fine just the way it is," they might say, or worse, "I want it to be like this. I don't want to change anything."

Even though it is incredibly tempting to move these students to the back of the line, the reality is, they are less likely to get instruction from teachers than any other students in your classroom. *Your most struggling student has probably had significantly more one-on-one time with teachers than your most sophisticated.*

Often these sophisticated writers deal with this issue of not-enough-teaching in a variety of ways. Some become approval seekers, following us around the classroom with paper in hand: "Is this good? Is this good?" Other students reject any and all tips that we might manage to squeak out when we do have the time to meet with them. Still others try desperately to fly below the radar, remain stubbornly quiet during shares, clearly working on their best attempts at becoming invisible during work times. There are of course other ways that strong writers present themselves, but it's important to keep in mind that these students need to be taught just as much as the other writers in our rooms.

Research has taught us that when strong students hit a certain age, if they are not challenged, they will actually lose abilities. According to the National Research Center on the Gifted and Talented, 20 percent of the high school dropout population (all races) were classified as gifted. Keep in mind that only approximately 6 percent of all students in the United States are classified as gifted according to the National Center for Education Statistics. Another sobering statistic: only 56 percent of students of color identified as gifted were still high achieving by the time they reached fifth grade, according to the Thomas Fordham Institute. The list goes on. We don't often think of our strongest students as being at risk of anything, but they are. It is important for students to know, actually for people of any age to know, that there is always more to learn, more to improve upon, more to strive for.

It is also worth knowing that working with these students is not the same as working with other students, at least when it comes to the area of writing (or whatever other areas they are stand-out strong in). They require different motivations, approaches, and possibly different strategies, depending on the student. Sometimes knowing that these students need different content and different approaches is enough to stop us in our tracks.

✳ Recognizing the Opportunity: Raising Our Teaching *and* Writing Levels

The good news is that there are many fascinating and rewarding things about teaching students who are strong writers. Many of these things you are already well aware of:

- They often actively help their peers.

- Their work is a great example to show other students.

- They don't require as much attention as students who are struggling with writing.

But there are other great things about these writers that you might not have considered before:

- They are the canary in the coal mine — if they don't get something we are trying to teach, no one is getting it.

- They challenge us to move past our own best knowledge and teaching and develop the newest and strongest work we can.

- They invent and discover new things and teach them to us.

When we have students like these, we can often choose when and how we want to teach them. We know they will meet grade standards. We know they will get great marks on their report cards. Even if we only meet with them once during a unit of study. They give us the gift of time because things are rarely an emergency with them. They also give us hope when things are crashing and burning in our classrooms. "Hey — at least *she* got it," we'll say to console ourselves.

But, I believe the greatest opportunity that these knock-your-socks-off writers give us is the opportunity to outgrow ourselves. Since they already know most, if not all, the writing strategies we might need, we need to learn more strategies. Since they already do so much of what we have taught, and need to be challenged in the ways they learn, so we have good reasons to try new teaching approaches and methods. These new strategies and teaching methods will lift our level of teaching for the sophisticated student, but will also widen our repertoire and lift it for all of our students.

✳ Experiment: Building a Better Toolbox

There are of course many things we already know to teach students. And this entire book will continue to add to your repertoire. It is also worth saying, that for many of us, the reason we struggle with high-level writers is that we don't feel like anything in our current toolbox will do the job. We need not only a new-sized socket wrench, but also a new saw, a new screwdriver . . . Well, perhaps not all new tools — some of them just retrofitted. Some of them just repurposed. But the point is, we need to look at our toolbox and refine and revise it if we want to reach everyone.

RECONSIDER YOUR STANCE

One of the things that can be tricky when working with sophisticated writers is the feeling that they are already doing so well. They are clearly already writing at least at, if not significantly above, grade level. Which, for some of us, might mean we feel hesitant to teach them anything. After all, do they really *need* to learn anything since they are already so ahead of the game? But the truth is, as all published professional authors know, there are always things to change, things to make better. That's what editors in the publishing industry are for. They give professional writers insights and suggestions to make their writing, already very strong, stronger yet. It's not that the writing isn't good, it's that the editor's job is to help make good writing the best it can be, to allow the writer to reach the farthest reaches of his potential.

Teachers can do this too for our strongest writers. We can take on the stance of the editor. We can look to a piece of writing and instead of seeing it as the excellent work of a ___-year-old, we can instead look at it as simply a piece of writing and see what ways we could help give some perspective and input to improve it, much like a professional editor helps a professional writer. We might ask ourselves, and our students, questions such as:

- Where could the writer be stronger?

- Are there places where it could be cut?

- Where is the writing most compelling? How could those places be extended? How could that writing influence the rest of the piece?

- What themes or ideas is the writer addressing? Are there ways to address those themes in more powerful ways?

GATHER TOOLS

Of course, the questions above are not enough to guide your teaching. Even if you were able to comfortably adopt an editorial stance all the time, there might come a time where you feel as if you've run out of questions to ask, guidance to give. In that case, it helps to not approach a conference (any conference, but especially a conference with a strong writer) empty-handed. Following are a few tools you might want to tuck under your arm before you wade in:

- *Mentor texts at varying levels.* Most of us typically have a few go-to mentor texts that are right at or just above our students' writing abilities. However, with stronger writers, you will want to up the ante considerably. Gather a few more mentor texts with significant work to study. Consider writers who write with more complexity, experimentally, or even writers who are writing for adults (but with age-appropriate content). Often offering fresh mentors who have new moves to study can help refresh your and your students' coffers. See Figure 2–1 for examples.

Figure 2–1 A Curated List of Possible Mentor Texts for Sophisticated Writers

Genre	If Your Whole Class Mentor Is Usually	You Might Try This
Personal Narrative	*Eleven* by Sandra Cisneros *Shortcut* by Donald Crews	"Everything Will Be Okay" by James Howe. *Risk-taking writing. Mature content. Reflections go into the future.* "The 1928 Packard" by Richard Peck. *Complex structure. Deep reflections connected to flashback.*
Fiction	*Fireflies!* by Julie Brinkloe "Mr. Entwhistle" by Jean Little "Spaghetti" by Cynthia Rylant	*Each Kindness* by Jacqueline Woodson. *Fiction that is painfully realistic. The ending is not a solution, but a way of raising more questions. The surprising use of weather, small details, and character actions is inspiring.* "Thirteen and a Half" by Rachel Vail. *Very funny story, that is also quite deep. Strong use of symbolism throughout; character development is subtle and strong.*
Persuasive Writing	*I Wanna an Iguana* by Karen Kaufman Orloff *The True Story of the 3 Little Pigs* by Jon Sceiszka	"Brothers" by Jon Scieszka. *A strong use of personal details and anecdotes to support a claim that comes at the end of the piece.* "Letter from a Birmingham Jail" by Rev. Dr. Martin Luther King. *Historical significance in persuasive writing that uses very specific examples and argument.* *Chew On This* by Charles Wilson and Eric Schlosser. *Incredibly persuasive writing that is also very informative and research-based. Great example of the power of word and evidence choice.*
Informational Texts	*The Adventures of a Plastic Bottle* by Alison Inches *Wolves* by Seymour Simon	*Elephants* by Steve Jenkins. *Strong structural work where the structure mimics the content. Also very strong use of metaphors.* *Robots* by Melissa Stewart. *Smooth, almost invisible, transitions between sentences, paragraphs, and chapters. Seamless integration between features and text.* *The Young People's History of the United States* by Howard Zinn. *Informational text with a strong angle. Obvious use of little-referred-to research. Strong example of showing multiple sides of a topic.*

- *Your own writing.* Your students at all levels of writing ability benefit from you writing and carrying your writing with you. This is no different for strong writers. The more you write, the more you will uncover strategies you can teach to students. In addition, you can use your own writing to experiment with fancier writing moves to teach stronger writers and share with them.

- *A cheat sheet.* This is the tool that keeps on giving no matter what student you are working with. However, most cheat sheets often only contain more generic, highly accessible strategies that can or must be taught. Ideally a cheat sheet for stronger writers would include more numerous unique writing tips and strategies. Ones that will feel new and challenging for the most jaded, been-there-done-that writer. Later in this chapter I will describe a few of my more commonly used teaching points, which can easily be made into a cheat sheet.

- *A sample of higher-level student writing.* Carrying a piece of higher-level student writing offers many teaching opportunities. It allows students to see what is possible for writers of their age. It helps remind us of things we might teach. It can also serve as a demonstration or practice text in a pinch.

SHARPEN THE UPPER REACHES OF YOUR WRITING KNOWLEDGE

None of the tools mentioned above are good for much if you still feel as if you don't have the depth of knowledge to refer to when teaching a smarty-pants writer. When you have time—even five minutes here and there will do—make a point of increasing your own knowledge about writing. In an ideal world you would be able to take a college-level course on writing. But, if that's not possible, you might consider any of the following:

- *Read more books on the teaching of writing.* There are countless books on the teaching of writing. If you don't already have them on your bookshelf, search out a few tried and true written by the masters: Murray, Graves, Calkins. These authors do an amazing job of not only addressing teaching, but also the work of writing. If you already know these books, consider widening your reach. The resource section on my website, www.colleencruz.com, lists some favorites.

- *Dig into books written for professional writers.* While the chances are pretty good that you have already read a few books for teachers of writing (you are holding this one, after all), it is more likely that you haven't read a ton of books simply about writing. There are countless books that professional writers, or people studying to be professional writers, refer to on a regular basis. They are chock-full of tips and suggestions for writing. Not all of the ideas are appropriate, or even accessible to children. However, many of them are, or else are easily adaptable. Start by choosing books that either address a variety of genres or else are focused on a genre you are studying with your students. One of my favorites for a general book about writing is Janet Burroway's *Creative Writing*. There is little doubt that by studying writing in this unexpected place you will find things to teach your strongest writers that they have never been exposed to before and will likely help push them to the next level.

- *Read more examples of the genres you plan to teach.* We know that it is good practice to have students immersed in the kinds of writing they are aiming to create. However, when's the last time you immersed yourself in examples of the genre you are planning to teach? Take some time to sit on the floor in your local library or bookstore and pore through the stacks. Look for as many examples as possible of the genre you are teaching, in as many different forms as possible (Picture book? Periodical? Anthology?). Don't shy away from examples from the adult section, or at readabilities higher or lower than your students' ability levels. You are looking for examples of the genre so you can gather as deep a sense of the genre as possible. Look for patterns across pieces. Find common structural choices, craft moves, even themes. These things will help feed your instruction in that genre, and will also make you feel more confident that you will have something to respond with, no matter what a strong writer can throw at you.

- *Work on your own writing in the genres you are teaching.* Donald Graves was one of the first to teach us that if we want students to write, we must write ourselves. Even more than that, we need to make that writing public. Since then, countless other educators, from Lucy Calkins to Penny Kittle to Carl Anderson to Ralph Fletcher, have reinforced this crucial point. Students, all students, need to see a more experienced practitioner work on his craft. This goes doubly so for strong writers because when they look to their peers for examples, they will find almost nothing they can emulate. I think we hesitate to use our own writing sometimes because we do not think it is worthy of our students' attention. It will be far less than perfect. But that is precisely the point. In our imperfections we learn where the struggles may lie as we come across them. We learn what is challenging about description in narrative, and how varying transitions in an essay can be taxing. When we choose to model, we also have texts where we can model how to revise and make stronger our pieces. Our students, especially our students who are used to being "naturally" good at something, need to see what it looks like when people they admire struggle and then how those admirable people deal with those struggles.

DESCRIBE WHAT THE WRITER IS DOING

When someone is a good writer, whether a child or an adult, they are used to compliments. They know they are good at what they do. And as they say in New York City, that and $2.50 will get you on the subway. Those general pieces of praise do nothing to move the writer to new heights. What can help is to see, really see, and to describe what is being seen to the writer. Instead of saying, "Great use of vocabulary!" push to say, objectively as possible, the things you see the writer actually doing. "Looking at this paragraph I see very precise nouns and verbs. Some of them really pop for me because they are so precise. They capture the essence of what's happening. You are also very sparing in your use of adjectives, which helps keep the prose clean. When you do use adjectives they are fresh and unexpected, such as here, when you describe Grandpa as 'mustachioed.'"

In that describing, a couple of things are likely to happen. First, the student will feel as if they are really seen. They will likely take this as a very sincere compliment, but also they will know that they can no longer hide behind smoke and mirrors. Second, you will likely find what you can teach the student the more you describe. You will notice the things that you are not saying as much about, or finding yourself sort of looking for things that you expect to be there that might not be as honed as you might have expected. You might also be able to best see what the student is gesturing toward but hasn't quite mastered. These are all possible sweet spots for teaching.

REACH FOR COMMON GO-TO TEACHING POINTS

Of course, it should go without saying that before teaching any student almost anything, we would want to first be sure that we have a strong sense of what they need and are ready to learn. That said, over the years I have found that there are a handful of very common go-to teaching points that I turn to again and again when working with sophisticated writers, because they are likely to have areas to work on with these topics. This is mainly because I have noticed common patterns in what many students have likely been taught (and probably mastered) before I work with them, and because I also know there are other topics that have likely been either overlooked or underpracticed.

- *Meaning and significance*

  Often sophisticated writers are so used to wowing the crowd with their fancy vocabulary and complex use of punctuation, that they spend less time considering the substance of their pieces—what some teachers call the "so what?" of writing. It is a very worthy thing to set students up with some guided practice in order to help them uncover the deeper meaning and significance of what they are trying to say in their pieces. One of the biggest challenges of this work is pushing them past platitudes and clichés into saying what they really are thinking and feeling. The idea of helping writers uncover and then develop the meaning and significance behind their writing is clearly not limited to those who find writing easier, but it is often the case that it can be more challenging to do this work with stronger writers who often feel as if their meaning is clear and understandable in all their writing.

  Additionally, before we teach almost anything else to help raise the level of a student's writing, we must first get to the significance of their writing, what Donald Graves called the heart, because the heart is what will drive all the other choices the writer might make to improve upon his own best work.

- *Structure*

  Most strong writers have a pretty strong handle on basic structural moves. They can organize a story into a nice arc. They can create clear thesis statements and support those statements with logically ordered evidence. They can create logical categories within informational writing. However, what they are less likely to have done is play with more complex and sophisticated structures. It is also likely that they have spent little time considering the ways that structure can set off meaning and vice versa. You might want to introduce students to a few alternative, less common structure types that can be used for a variety of genres.

  - *Framing structures are structures where there is an outer structure and an inner structure.* The outer structure is often, but not always, a story, which frames the inner, main part of the piece. An example of this would be *The Princess Bride*, with the story of the boy and his grandfather setting off the story of Wesley and Buttercup.

  - *Flash back or flash forward.* What's nice about pieces that are structured this way is that they allow for showing and not telling (in narratives) about motivations and resolutions. In essays, they allow for some reflections without expostulation.

- *Inevitable but surprising endings.* At first glance, this may seem as if I am only talking about crafting an ending, and not structure at all. But when readers are surprised by an ending, no matter if it's an informational piece, an essay, a poem, or a story, there is usually a structure, starting from the very first line, that led up to it. Teaching students to plan their pieces backwards, thinking of where they want to leave the reader, can often lead to some very sophisticated structures.

- *Mix structures and genres.* Advanced writers can see shades of gray. We can show students how they can combine various structures and genre trappings in order to get a greater effect. For example, informational writing can borrow from narrative by building suspense (see Melissa Stewart's *No Monkeys, No Chocolate*).

- **Strong language usage** (economy of language, nouns and verbs, cracking open a word) Starting in fifth grade, all the way through high school, I often found that my writing was graded by pounds, rather than by content. What I mean by that was that teachers would assign page numbers for assigned pieces and I would have to strive to make that minimum requirement if I hoped to get a decent grade. The problem was, I was a very economical writer. I still am. I could say in a few words what could have been said in many more—and probably often was. Unfortunately, the teachers in my life (and likely in many of our students' lives) reinforced the notion that a certain number of words or pages was just as important, if not more important, than the content. Page counts encourage fluff and bluster and very, very, very many more words than are really necessary. Strong writers are perhaps the most vulnerable to this type of misguided expectation. You ask—they do.

  Unfortunately this leads to some bad habits: overuse of adjectives and adverbs, passive verb tenses, asides and setups meant to invoke voice (if you know what I mean). We will all do our students a huge favor if we teach them to use adjectives and adverbs sparingly. I teach students that they are like the salt and saffron of writing, respectively. A little goes a long way and can bring out the flavors in the writing. Too much and it can ruin everything.

  You might be wondering how writing can possibly be beautiful, let alone precise, without these two parts of speech used copiously. Allow me to make a case for strong nouns and verbs. Try this little activity for yourself. Take this sentence and try to rewrite it with only nouns and verbs (no adjectives or adverbs): *The beautiful woman walked slowly through the gorgeous room.*

What did you come up with? I came up with:

- The bombshell strutted through the gallery.

- The duchess glided through the cathedral.

Both sentences are tighter and shorter than the original. But, perhaps more importantly, they are more precise. They give you a very clear picture of exactly what the author was hoping you would picture.

While I would argue that all students deserve more direct instruction into the use of strong nouns and verbs and less on adjectives and adverbs, for our most sophisticated writers, this becomes crucial because it often flies in the face of what they think makes writing good.

Additionally, we might teach them Georgia Heard's strategy of cracking open a word. This strategy entails taking a word or phrase, like "My mom is altruistic" (don't be fooled by the fancy vocabulary!) and making it more accurate by not only thinking of synonyms, but also images, metaphors, anecdotes. So that I could instead be writing, "Mom is the kind of person who knows that when you're sick you want nothing more than tomato soup and a nap on the couch with her comforter tucked in all around you." Or, "I was getting up in the middle of the night to go to the bathroom when I saw Mom, wearing her pajamas, putting more stuffing into my teddy bear and sewing him back up. I didn't know he was even missing." (See Figure 2–2.)

- *Metaphor and symbolism*
Once students have a strong sense of meaning and significance, it's just a hop, skip, and jump to working on developing metaphors and symbolism. What's great about this work, is that although it feels extra-fancy, it is also work that we can easily teach to the whole class. When teaching metaphor we can teach students to think in terms of the idea they are trying to convey and some of its characteristics. Then move from that to thinking of something concrete that has a few of those characteristics. So, if I was thinking I wanted to describe my mother's love, I would think about how it's always there, I almost take it for granted. It's simple, yet beautiful. I can then think of objects that have some of those characteristics—like oxygen. It's always there, simple, yet one cannot imagine life without it.

- *Tension and suspense*
When writers have a strong sense of story, one of the things they can do is up the tension and suspense. Noah Lukeman has many great strategies for doing this in his book for professional writers, *The Plot Thickens*. A few of my favorites, and easiest to teach, include increasing the characters' motivation (the more a character wants

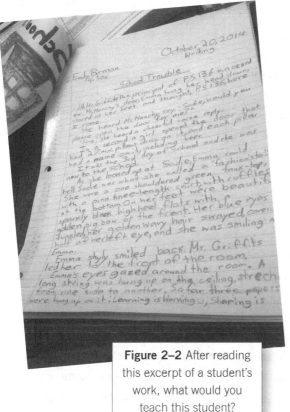

Figure 2–2 After reading this excerpt of a student's work, what would you teach this student?

School Trouble

As Mr. Griffits, the principal of P.S. 136 knocked on Ms. Henchy's door, Emma hung her head down, stared at her feet and thought, P.S. 136, here I come.

She heard Ms. Henchy say, "Sadie, would you please open the door for me?"

"Sure," she heard a cheerful voice reply.

In a second a girl opened the door that had 27 mini pillows drawn on it, and each pillow had a name on it, including hers.

It was the 3rd day of school and she was new to the school.

As she looked up at Sadie, Emma could tell Sadie was what she called a "fashionista". She wore a one shouldered green tank-top, with a pink knee-length skirt, with ruffles at the bottom. On her feet were beautiful sparkly black high heel flats with a golden big bow at the front. Her blue eyes twinkled, her golden wavy hair swayed, covering half of her left eye, and she was smiling at Emma.

Emma shyly smiled back. Mr. Griffits led her to the front of the room.

Emma's eyes gazed around the room. A long string was hung up on the ceiling, streching from one side to another. So far three papers were hung up on it: Learning is Working, Sharing is Caring and the school motto: WORK HARD, BE KIND!

something, the more the reader is invested in what happens), increase the danger (physical, mental, emotional), or create limits (confined in space, shortened time, inability to act, etc.).

- *Research* (finding more information from other sources—even for fiction)
  It often surprises kids to learn that writers, almost all writers, research something before they finish writing a piece. They typically imagine that research only applies to writers of information texts. But, a great thing we can teach them is to research, no matter what they are writing. Poets can research history, or the scientific terms for a unique form of bug life. Fiction writers can research grocery-store protocol or ingredients for a great lemon meringue pie. And essayists should research to make sure their evidence is valid and that they are not missing some key point that will make their piece more convincing. We can show them how to research fast, and then how to incorporate their findings seamlessly into a piece in a way that befits the genre.

- *Weight*

    All writers should have something, or a few somethings, that matter most in a given piece. However, perhaps because many of us are egalitarian, most of the amount of space taken up, actual word count dedicated to that importance, is often equal to the word count of other subsidiary points. We can teach writers that when they are writing about anything, they want to make sure that the longest sections, or the most actual words, are dedicated to the things that matter most to them. If the fight is the whole point in the story, then this should take several paragraphs, if not pages, to show. If one piece of evidence is the most compelling in the essay, then that should be the longest one.

✳ Make Independent Writing Projects a Priority

The most organic, strongest, writing workshop classrooms often have independent writing projects at their heart. That is, students are following the whole-class curriculum, but they are also cultivating and moving through the writing process with a piece of their own design. In other words, a student might be working on her literary essay in the whole-class unit, but she might also be working on a historical-fiction short story during her writing free time. She, and the rest of the students, have learned how to plan and implement their own writing projects, moving through their writing process independently, applying all that they have learned and are learning in the class writing workshop. I write more about this later in this book, as well as in my book *Independent Writing*, so I'm not going to go into too much detail here. Except to say, that independent writing projects can be a lifeline for so many strong writers who do not feel challenged or interested (whether rightly or not) by their class's writing curriculum. Often, when students have independent writing projects they start to become more invested in the whole-class curriculum because they care so much about their independent projects.

✳ Ongoing Work: Plan for Acceleration

The thing about sophisticated writers—or students who are sophisticated in any subject—be it math, technology, or fashion—is that their learning never slows down. In fact, month after month, if we are doing our jobs right, they will be accelerating their learning, and we might very well feel like we're chasing after them. One way to head off this feeling is to spend a few minutes making a writing teaching plan for these students. I am sure you have many of these for your class, often organized around goals, strengths, and weaknesses. Howcvcr, I know many of us don't always make a very detailed learning plan for our strongest writers, so busy are we planning to move the students who need to move right away.

However, if we make a plan—it doesn't have to be a fancy one, where we envision a few courses of study for our strongest students over the course of a unit or a semester, or even a year—we might have enough of a big picture of where we want to go that even if we don't meet these students that often, there will still be continuity. For example, I could decide that since Kanika is at or above grade level in almost all her writing skills, I can start looking toward the next year's standards to set her goals. I might make sure there is a sprinkling of higher-level grammar and conventions, as well as some fancier structural work and more attention to meaning (the last is not really standards-based, but definitely vital). I would definitely have a discussion with Kanika about her own goals for herself. Then I might make a plan for her for the year, including a few students who have similar trajectories for the year. It could look like Figure 2–3.

Figure 2–3 Learning Trajectories for Advanced Students

Goals	Unit 1— *Narrative*	Unit 2— *Editorials*	Unit 3— *Information*	Unit 4— *Fiction*	Unit 5— *Poetry*	Unit 6— *Lit. Essay*	Unit 7— *Journalism*
Syntactical complexity	X			X			
Structure connected to meaning			X		X		X
Language		X				X	

The idea isn't that I'm planning out all the minutia of every time I meet with Kanika, but rather that she and I share a plan for her learning together. We will get to the actual teaching points as we get closer to the teaching. Even if all it adds up to is six tailored sessions in the course of a school year, these sessions will still be crucial for ensuring that Kanika isn't overlooked, or worse yet, avoided because I don't know what to teach her.

3

"I can't seem to get my students to stay writing unless I'm sitting beside them."

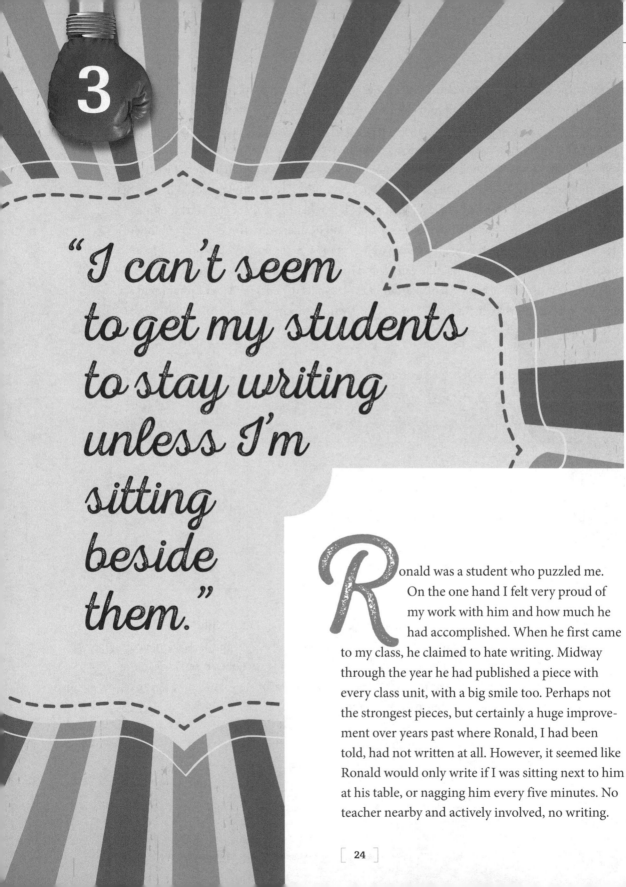

Ronald was a student who puzzled me. On the one hand I felt very proud of my work with him and how much he had accomplished. When he first came to my class, he claimed to hate writing. Midway through the year he had published a piece with every class unit, with a big smile too. Perhaps not the strongest pieces, but certainly a huge improvement over years past where Ronald, I had been told, had not written at all. However, it seemed like Ronald would only write if I was sitting next to him at his table, or nagging him every five minutes. No teacher nearby and actively involved, no writing.

It didn't take me long to realize that I had started to make a writer out of Ronald, but one who was dependent on me. And while, theoretically, it was a huge improvement over what Ronald had done in the past, and he was certainly strengthening his writing muscles more by writing than by not writing, I also knew that he wasn't truly growing as a writer unless he could write without me. After all, eventually he would leave my classroom, and there were no guarantees that future teachers would be willing to work side-by-side with this student to be sure he produced.

Unfortunately, Ronald is not the only student I have worked with, whether as a classroom teacher or as a staff developer, who has developed into a dependent writer. It's an insidious thing because as teachers we feel compelled to make sure a student makes as much progress as he can in his learning and are willing to do whatever it takes to make it happen. And, if I'm completely honest, it can feel very good to have a student show marked progress and growth because of my presence. On the other hand, we also know that if a child is dependent on us and cannot apply his learning independently, that is problematic.

✳ Why It Can Stop Us: When Something We Know Is Wrong Feels Right

In my opinion, there are few things in this life that feel as good as helping another person. One of the reasons many of us became a teacher was to help others. So, when we pull up a chair alongside a struggling writer and she produces as we sit shoulder to shoulder, there is something that warms our spirits. And, truthfully, there is and should be space in every writer's workshop for writing teachers to sit side-by-side with their students and write with them.

However, it becomes a problem when a student is *only* writing when we are right beside them. There are a few things that make it tough to stop oversupporting students, or to stop the atmosphere in the classroom that accommodates oversupport from the other adults in the room as well.

For one thing, this can be an invisible problem. What we see isn't much to look at. When we or another adult sit with the child, they produce. When we don't sit next to them, they stop. Therefore, it can be hard to spot that spending a lot of time with a student can actually do more harm than just letting them struggle a bit, or teaching them strategies to help them work on more of their struggles independently. In the short term it can be easier to sit with a student and ensure that he works on his writing than it is to constantly nudge, prompt, deflect, and teach multiple strategies. As anyone who has ever helped a preschooler get ready for school knows, it is so much easier, and faster, to just put the danged shoe on for him than to let him do it himself. It's tough to admit, but sometimes we're just so overwhelmed, tired, or busy and it's just easier to sit with a kid than to not.

If you are currently helping a student a little too much, and have decided it's time to pull back, you might find that old habits are hard to break. You have built a routine of working with this student and the relationship as well as the routine would have to change. Compound that with the fact that many students don't want the support to end. Just as an infant balks at having to lift his own spoon to his mouth, many of our students would prefer to have a teacher sit beside them and support them every time they write. They have often received this level of support, or something like it, their entire schooling career, and the idea of having to work harder isn't always appealing. As part of that cycle, many students slide back and struggle more. Whether it is an attempt to get us to come back, or simply because they don't yet have the tools they need to support their own writing life, if we do try to pull away, many of our students will actually regress and struggle more than they did before we started to support them. It can be challenging to look at that backslide and not return to the habits we had before.

And, if that wasn't a sticky enough situation, there are sometimes other adults in the equation who don't want the current level of support to end. Sometimes administrators appreciate that students who were once deemed troublemakers are now well in hand. Assistant teachers and paraprofessionals can have a clear task to accomplish with certain students. Service providers can feel confident that a student's IEP goals are being worked on constantly. Parents and other caregivers often appreciate the extra attention their children are receiving. To be clear, none of these people have bad motives. However, we should acknowledge that when other adults are working with a child, we don't feel required to coordinate our work with theirs so that we're collaborating on student independence. Dealing with the other adults in this student's life can simply compound the difficulties.

Finally, and I mentioned this earlier, but it bears repeating since I think it can be the toughest obstacle—it feels good to help others. And at first glance, oversupporting a student can feel as if we are helping them. We can look down at their pages filled with writing and know that we were a big part of that work. Unfortunately, this is a false sense of help.

✳ Recognizing the Opportunity: Our Students Need to Learn Independence While They Still Have a Safety Net

In many ways it is simpler and less painful for a teacher to continue to offer a student endless support, whether the student needs it or not. True, we might be aware that we are only enabling bad habits, but it is very likely that there will be no major consequences for us, at least while they are still students in our class. And it is so hard to help students become independent learners when they don't want to be. However, if we don't view the reduction of support as a means of marooning a child, but rather equipping him with survival skills while he's still on the boat, we can see that this is a perfect time to work toward independence.

When we are constantly hovering over a student, or in a worst-case scenario actually do the writing work for him, we are not able to see what a student can actually achieve independently throughout the writing process. When we step back a bit and observe, we can determine what a student's strengths are and where he might need additional strategies to try.

We know from recent work, such as the research of Carol Dweck, that children need to learn the importance of effort and the power of learning from one's failures. If our young writers rarely get to experience that uncomfortable butt-in-seat feeling, where writing is challenging and might not even work right, we are taking away an opportunity for them to learn that they can fail and still be okay. In fact, in writing as it is with many other disciplines, often the best ideas come from the failures. By not letting them fail, we can ironically undermine the very self-confidence we are trying to protect.

Of course, one of the biggest reasons we want students to develop as much independence as possible is because eventually they will leave us. If we taught in a one-room schoolhouse and we would teach the student from K to college, then perhaps an argument could be made that giving a student all the support she wants is fine. However, for almost all of us, there will come a time when the school year will end and the student will move out of our care and into the care of another educator. We want that student to know as much about writing as they possibly can so that they can be successful no matter where they go next. So, while we might consider what we are doing to support a child temporary, we need to make sure it is really temporary under our watch.

For all of the above-mentioned reasons, students need to be able to write independently. They also need to be able to write independently because as long as they are still relying on us to complete the most basic of writing tasks, we have not done our jobs. As Carl Anderson has said, batting coaches don't stand at the plate and bat for the player. Rather, they know they've done their jobs well when the players are able to bat without them.

✳ Experiment: Mindfully Handing Over the Reins

The exciting thing about working on developing independence is that what you are working toward is very black and white. If you decide to go for it, you will immediately discover if you are doing something to enable a student or empower him because he will either need you less, or else he will need you the same amount (or more!).

The first step I believe is the most crucial. It is not so much an action as a stance. We need to assume competence. This was something my teaching partner, Jenifer Taets, taught me years ago, and was further seconded by Kara Gustafson, a special education consultant. The idea is simple. Before we swoop down to offer students tons of support, we should see what they can do independently. As Kristine Mraz, master teacher and co-author of *Smarter*

Charts, has been known to say, "I pretend I can't use my arms. If I let them try to do everything, it might not be perfect, it will probably be messy, but most kids will figure out how to do a lot more than we think they can." We should assume, and make visible our assumption, that she can do a lot more than we know and then actively observe to get a sense of what a student can and can't do. If, after letting her have a go at something, she struggles too much — to the point of frustration, then dole out support, slowly, until they are no longer frustrated and are now back to being appropriately challenged.

As part of that effort, we will want to apply the least restrictive, most tailored scaffolding. When I was a new teacher, I am embarrassed to admit, I used to claim to support my strugglers by handing out graphic organizers. Every student who had a hard time with writing would receive the same graphic organizer. Some students did have trouble with organization, but for others it was a fine-motor issue; still others struggled with generating ideas. So for one or two kids my scaffolds worked, but for most they did nothing — or even worse, they held some writers back. Now I know that if I am going to use scaffolding, I need to make sure it matches the individual student's needs and still allows her to work at her maximum capacity.

Additionally, when putting a scaffold in place, we need to concurrently have a plan for how and when to remove it. Scaffolding on buildings and in teaching is meant to be temporary. Just as construction companies put up scaffolding with a timeline for removal, we need to do the same. When a child needs a scaffold to support her, we need to provide what she needs. Perhaps she needs a list of sentence frames she can use to get started. Perhaps she needs to always rehearse her writing orally before she records it. Whatever the scaffold is, when you introduce it to the child, you might consider saying to the student that you are giving them a tool they will use for a few weeks (days, minutes) to help them get stronger at a skill they want to strengthen. Then, perhaps to keep yourself honest, set an alarm on your phone or computer to remind you when you should pull the scaffold back a bit. Then another alarm for removing that scaffold. That way, even if the student isn't yet ready for the removal, you are reminded that it needs to go eventually.

Of course, not all supports need be temporary. School is a great time to teach interdependence in order to support independence. After all, once they leave school, it is most likely their friends and colleagues who will support them with their life goals. Therefore, we need to teach students how to work well with their peers. Being able to work well with peers is one of those gifts that keep on giving. The thing is, students don't always know how to do this effectively. You might consider teaching a string of lessons to your whole class on how to give strong feedback and support to their writing partners.

Not every reason a student seems to need an adult to prod him has to do with learning difficulties. Sometimes the reason a student is struggling so hard with his writing is that he is not engaged with it. The genre or the purpose or the topic is just not compelling to him. If that is the case, you might want to refer to Chapters 5, 6, and 12 for ideas and strategies for working with disengaged writers. You might also consider adding independent projects to your curriculum. When students are able to develop and implement their own independent writing projects concurrently with the whole-class curriculum, there is often energy to spare in terms of writing across the day with more volume and interest. Because students are so invested in say, their comic book, they will want to learn more about how story arcs go and character development so that they can apply those things to the projects of their own invention. As I mention elsewhere, I write about this extensively in my book *Independent Writing* (2004), so I won't get into the details here. Suffice it to say, when students are working on independent writing projects, they are doing them alongside of the whole-class writing curriculum. Sort of like how students will have independent books they are reading during your mystery unit, in addition to mystery ones. So your class might be studying poetry, but when a student has free time, for homework, or at designated independent project times, students will work on their fantasy stories, plays, and newspaper articles.

You might also consider offering seminars once a month or once a week. Seminars are when students learn from each other or guest teachers about a topic of interest. Usually students either request a topic or someone volunteers to teach it. Other students then sign up for the seminar on a given day. Seminars have the dual purpose of empowering students to share their learning with others and to play the role of teacher, as well as allowing even more choice and offering alternative voices for the attendees of the seminars. (See Figure 3–1.) There is something fantastic about watching students teach what they've been learning in writing workshop, as well as what they've invented. The amount of attention to detail they put into teaching can help us see where our teaching is strongest, and where it might need shoring up. Additionally, when students lead and sign up for seminars it further reinforces interdependence.

✳ Ongoing Work: Keeping the Student from Slipping Back into Dependence

If you see this, first try not to panic. It's entirely possible that the student is just having a slight setback. It's also possible that there's no setback at all, the student is merely in a generative stage and is doing more work in her head than on paper. Give the student a bit of time, and perhaps a friendly check-in. If the student doesn't get back on track, you might consider having a heart-to-heart, transparent conversation where you put everything on the table.

You might just say something along the lines of, "Ronald, at the beginning of the year you had a lot of support from grownups with your writing. But you grew so much and can do so

Figure 3–1 Student Seminar Poster

much by yourself. Yet, lately I haven't seen that same work showing up. What's been going on that's getting in the way of the kind of writing you and I know you can do?" By having this conversation I've often found most solutions are fairly simple. I've also discovered that some students perk right up when they remember how much they already can and have done, and were simply slipping into bad habits.

Another option is to make an actual study, for just yourself, yourself and some willing colleagues, perhaps even you and your students, where you focus on what makes students independent writers. You can examine the classroom environment, the roles of adults and children in the classroom, tools and resources provided, even curricular decisions. You are looking to see where students are independent, where they are interdependent, where they are dependent. From there you might want to chip away at the places where students are still dependent — especially places where they don't need to be. For example, no upper-grade teacher should still be holding the keys to the paper and pens. If students want to write, and need paper, they should be able to access it without an adult. Take a walk, virtual or otherwise, through your classroom, looking for all the places you could up the independence quotient.

This is big and ongoing work, as there is always something more that students can and should do independently.

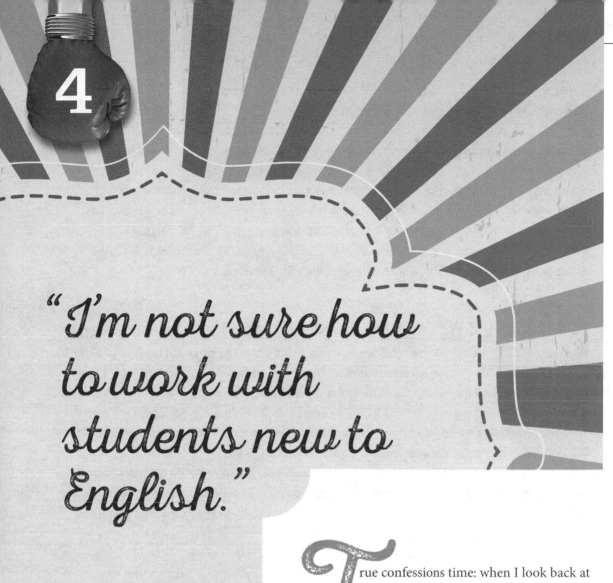

4

"I'm not sure how to work with students new to English."

True confessions time: when I look back at my years in the classroom, there were students I can point to that I know I didn't do enough for.

Yes, I loved them and surrounded them with literature and made sure they were in a classroom that supported risk-taking and independence. I did that for everyone. But I know that there are certain kids whose individual needs I just was not prepared to meet. Those are the students I wish I could call and apologize to. Let them know I did the best I could but I know it wasn't good enough. One of those students was a boy I'll call Sameer.

Sameer came into my classroom a couple of months into the school year. He was dressed in freshly pressed clothes and was walked to the classroom door by his father and our principal. He had just moved to the United States from Yemen to join his father and older brothers, but leaving behind his mother and younger siblings. When I smiled and said hello at the door, Sameer looked up at me and gave me the sweetest smile I had ever seen. "He doesn't speak any English," his father apologized. "I'm so glad he's joining us," I said, not really responding to his father's information. I shepherded Sameer into the room and introduced him to his classmates, smiling the whole time. But inside, my heart was pounding and I could already feel sweat breaking out on my forehead and back. I had no idea what I was going to do to teach a student whose language I literally knew not a word of.

✳ What Stops Us: We Focus on Not Knowing the Student's Language

So much of teaching is building relationships and making connections with students. I like to share things I have in common with them. I like to tell jokes. I love to hear about their hopes and fears and tap those to help me tailor my instruction to them. When I don't know a student's primary language, I often feel as if some of my best tools are outside of my reach. It's a horribly selfish perspective, but it is true that one of the things that can be tough about having a student who is learning English in your classroom is having to learn new tools when so many of the ones I have used in the past have worked for me. Add to that, often students who speak different languages come from cultures I might not know so well. Which means there are also cultural mores and traditions that I know little about. I might misstep or offend when I am trying to reach.

Another challenge, which seems to be getting bigger every day, is the need to balance English language learning with grade-level instructional expectations. When I first taught Sameer, years ago, as challenging as it was for me at times to figure out how to teach him the grade curriculum and ensure that he had lots of language supports and practice, there was little in terms of high-stakes testing for him. In fact, he wouldn't need to take the state tests for a few more years. This is not the case in many places today, where some schools' success is being measured by the growth of English language learners among other cohorts of students. When this pressure occurs, some teachers confess to feeling frustrated and say they end up not focusing as much on the language-learning aspects as perhaps they should, instead opting for teaching things that will show up on assessments of the school's progress. For people who manage to place that pressure aside and instead focus singularly on what the student needs most, there is still the knowledge that a choice was made, one that might have consequences for you, and possibly for the student, depending on the nature of where you teach.

And then there's the very real chance that you do not have only one student who is studying to become bilingual. You might have several, each on different stages of language acquisition. In some schools, you could very well have multiple students each speaking different languages. In one Queens classroom I worked in, the teacher had thirteen different home languages being spoken by her students learning English. This was both intimidating and thrilling — imagine an eight-year-old having access to and picking up pieces of so many different languages!

Also tough is knowing the pace with which a student should be progressing. Since every student learns differently and at different paces always, teachers are used to the ways in which learners can be speeding up or lagging a bit and still very much not be raising any red flags. However, when a student is learning a new language, acclimating to a new country, *and* learning a new curriculum, it can be harder still to see if a student might have some disconnects in learning that could use additional services and supports. No teacher wants to be the one to suggest a student needs special education services because he is simply working at his own pace. On the other hand, we also don't want to be the teacher who has allowed a student to struggle for too long when a little boost of concentrated support could be just what he needs to make progress.

Finally, to be clear, this is definitely one of those topics in which I very much consider myself an active learner and studier, and I suspect it's that way for many of you as well. Yes, that's true of all the topics in this book; however, when it comes to students who are learning English, I feel as if this is a topic where almost anyone for whom it is not their primary area of expertise will need to continue to study for the length of their career. I know that even after almost twenty years of on-and-off study I very much feel as if I've just skimmed the surface. This is a rich and complex topic that needs to be visited and revisited time and again. Every day new research on best practices comes out. We will want to be sure to build on that research, while also making sure to not overly rely on a program that only teaches language at one time of the day, missing the opportunity to build rich language experiences across the school day.

There are countless languages being spoken and brought to our classrooms, and, as the world grows ever smaller, the need for deeper and more comprehensive understanding of what it means to learn a new language while simultaneously learning other new skills and content will likely become one of the most pressing issues in education.

✳ See Opportunity: The Value of More Than One Way of Communicating

When my father was a child, going to Kindergarten for the first time in the 1940s, speaking any language other than English was a severe disadvantage for a child. My father was actually beaten by his Kindergarten teacher if she overheard him using Spanish. The world was immersed in a world war and xenophobia was common. Fast forward to the twenty-first century with its global economy, and there are few things better in terms of employability and general worldliness than speaking more than one language. Being bilingual is a *huge* advantage. It is so much of an advantage that some of the highest-performing countries in terms of education make second (and third and fourth) language learning a top priority. The parents in the top economic tiers in the United States make certain their children learn at least one foreign language before they leave high school.

I believe this high value placed on second-language learning is very important to remember.

Somewhere along the way, students who are learning English have come to be seen by many educators as strugglers who might bring down a school's performance numbers, who will somehow be more difficult to teach than other students. "I have a lot of English language learners," I'll hear a teacher say as a way to explain why things aren't going well in his classroom. It's a funny thing. When I'm at a party and a friend says, "I decided to learn German," I see it as impressive. When someone is learning English, I feel like it would do all of us a lot of good, especially the child, if we were excited about it. What an advantage this student is going to have growing up!

And let's not fail to mention — what a boon for the whole class! A student with knowledge of a language different than the dominant language allows us all to learn about our own language structures, to learn about another language or culture if the student is willing to share, and reminds us all to think of a variety of ways to communicate and express ourselves. In classrooms where students learning English are embraced, there is often a lot of music, art, role-playing, and language play. It's not that those things can't and don't exist in classrooms with different populations, it is just that it's more likely to happen in places where people need to try to communicate with each other in a variety of ways.

For me, one of the biggest advantages (which is often the case when I learn how to teach a child who has needs that are new for me) is that I must learn new strategies and techniques. I can't rely on my tried-and-true ways of being in front of the classroom when I know there are students who will be less likely to learn that way. I must reach past my comfort zone. For example, I am the kind of teacher who often relies on my humor, but when I was working with students in Tokyo, I realized my wordplay was getting lost. I decided I could either tap another source of humor (silly images, pratfalls, etc.) or I could try engaging students in other ways. In this case I turned toward music and other types of pop culture that students could connect with. I was a stronger teacher for having reached outside of my familiar bag of tricks. And now I have a few new ones I can use across the globe. This move that I made, while being the language outsider, was something that I had to do in order to make sure I was being understood and that I was understanding others. Our goal is for our students to also do the same thing: we want to teach them strategies for communicating in order to make sure they are being understood and that they are understanding what is being communicated.

✳ Experiment: Build Off Students' Levels of Language Acquisition

The most important thing, of course, before we even consider the student's level of language understanding, is to get to know the student as a person. You will want to be aware of the language standards and guidelines that your state may have adopted and put out. Many states follow the WIDA Consortium's ELD Standards, including Illinois and Massachusetts, while others states, like California and New York, have developed their own, which use distinct verbiage to refer to the stages of language acquisition. This, of course, is important for all students. However, since many of our students who are learning English are immigrants, we will also want to do some preliminary work getting to know something of the country they are from. We might want to find out: the culture of that country, whether they are from an urban, suburban, or rural area, what economic background the student might have had, and if that has shifted since emigrating. Additionally, we might want to read books, such as *One Green Apple* by Eve Bunting or *My Name Is María Isabel* by Alma Flor Ada, to help open up conversations about language, family backgrounds, and community.

From there you will want to begin to consider a clearer plan into language learning. It seems important to acknowledge that despite the fact that almost 10 percent of students in the United States are English language learners (some states, like California, have an average of 23 percent of its student population identified as English language learners), solid practices around supporting English language learners are not widely available in staff development and even in preservice certification programs. That said, whenever we're experimenting, we want to start with some reliable resources to ensure that our experiments are as worthwhile, efficient, and effective as possible. We don't want to waste time creating things that have already been created.

Perhaps the first thing you'll want to do is identify what level of language acquisition a student is at. (See Figure 4–1.) Once you know that, you can make a lot of decisions of the sorts of supports, curricular decisions, and the like that will make the most sense for your

Figure 4–1 Stages of Language Acquisition

Adapted from the work of Stephen Krashen and Tracy Terrell

Stage	Characteristics	Possible Strategies to Teach
Pre-production	Language learners are taking in a lot of vocabulary through listening. There might be some speaking, but it might not always be audible to the teacher. Learner might nod or use gestures. This stage varies in length from a few days to several months.	• Writers can rehearse their writing by sketching pictures and labeling with the words they know, as well as using dictionaries and partners. • Writers can listen to other people tell their stories, and think about how they might create a story of their own.
Early Production	Language learners are learning up to 1,000 words during this stage, which can last about six months. They might speak some words and phrases; however, they might not be in standard English.	• Writers can use sentence structures to help build their writing pieces. They might practice saying these sentences first, and then record them. • Writers take risks in their language. They draft as fast as they can, knowing that they can always go back and fix things up later.
Speech emergence	During this stage, language learners acquire a few thousand words. They often begin to be able to speak, read, write, and understand short sentences and questions.	• Writers know that there are different kinds of sentences. They consider ways to end those sentences (periods, question marks, exclamation points) in order to make sure they are saying what they want to say. • Writers can build longer sentences by combining two or more ideas. They can use words like *and*, *but*, or *or* to show how two ideas can go together.
Intermediate fluency	Learners at this stage might have several thousand words in their vocabulary. They are also able to understand and produce more complex sentences. This stage has been identified as being crucial in part because this is often the stage when language learners begin to think in their new language.	• Writers don't just write the first word that comes to their minds. They revise thinking if another word would be more accurate or better for a particular idea. • Writers revise to make sure that what they are thinking is what is on the page. They reread their writing to see if their words match their intentions. • Writers study professional writers to see if there are craft moves professional writers make that they can apply to their own work.
Advanced fluency	This is perhaps the longest stage learners stay at. That is because while it can take two years to reach this stage, it is believed that it can take at least a decade for mastery of a second language.	• Writers consistently outgrow their own best work. They study the last thing they wrote, name the work they did well, then consider ways to make their best piece build on those moves and improve upon them. • Writers work to include nuances of meaning. They understand that words, phrases, and ideas can have multiple interpretations. Using description, evidence, and argument, they make sure to bring complexity to their work.

students. Just like with all learners, we want to be sure we are scaffolding just enough so that students are not feeling frustration, but not so much that they are bored and have no work to do. For those reasons we want to be very clear on what our students need before we begin to implement our ideas.

Perhaps one of the fastest ways to support students who are learning English, as well as learners who just prefer visual communication, is to tap into more visual means of communicating. I know when I travel to countries where I am learning the language, I rely heavily on visual clues. This can include ideas such as:

- Classroom objects labeled with photographs, drawings, and words. (See Figure 4–2.) These can be done with photographs, clip art, and label-makers. No object should be left unlabeled! Some teachers like to add a sentence under the label as a way to put the word in context. So, for example, under the label *pens*, there might be a sentence like "We use **pens** for writing." Or "May I use a **pen** in writing today?"

- Instructional charts using icons, which are repeated across not just the classroom but also the grade and the school. For example, the icon for book would be the same whether in the school library or in the science lab. This helps build consistency for language access points across a building, which can be helpful for students as they move through their days and years in a building.

Figure 4–2 Labels

- Instructional charts that are written in a step-by-step format. This allows students at earlier stages of language acquisition to visually cue into what is expected and the way to use the strategy. Attaching a physical representation of a writing piece next to each step is an even clearer way for those students to make meaning and encourage practice. (See Figure 4–3.)

Figure 4–3 Writing Process Instructional Chart

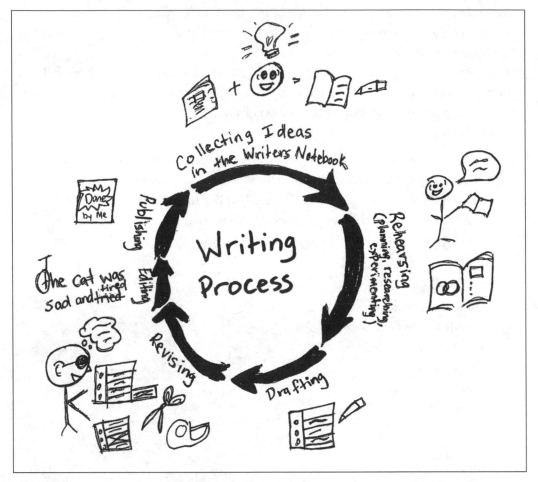

- Incorporate more gestures into your teaching and encourage students to do the same in their conversations. For example, using one hand gesture for reading, and another for writing, can help students start to connect the actions with the words. I am also a big believer in overacting. I try to use over-the-top facial expressions and motions all the time — not just when I have language learners in my crowd. I find that these help all students to attend, and for students with all kinds of learning needs, these gestures can be helpful. The key is to try to keep the gestures as consistent as possible — just as we would want to do with icons.

- Color-coding folders, chart marker colors, even bulletin board backing paper so that subjects have colors connected to them: writing — purple, reading —

red, math — blue, science — green, etc. can help keep unnecessary explanations to a minimum. It is also helpful for students to at least start with the correct materials, and be looking in the right general direction when trying to approximate classroom work.

Another great resource to tap in the service of supporting students who are learning English while also working on developing their writing skills is peer groupings. Most writing workshop classrooms have strong partnerships that support each other's goals, give feedback, and are also a sounding board. Many other classrooms also have writing clubs or writing response groups that enlarge the partnerships into groups of three to five students. When considering the best ways to group students to maximize their benefits, you might consider instead of partnerships for students who are learning English, having students in triads. This is especially helpful if there is another student in the class who speaks the same dominant language as the student who is newer to the language.

One popular triad makeup includes the student newer to English, a student who is bilingual in English and the language learner's dominant language, and one student who is English dominant. This allows for the student who is strongly bilingual to be able to practice both of her languages, while also getting support on her English writing work. The student who is English dominant gets exposure to another language, as well as a writing partner who can support his work. The new English speaker has an opportunity to hear and read English in a small-group environment, practice it in a less threatening space, and still have the support of someone who speaks her dominant language.

There are of course countless other ways to combine students into supportive writing relationships. No matter which way you decide to go, you will want to make sure that the new English speaker is supported, but so is any other student who is in the mix. We certainly do not want other students to be placed permanently into the role of translator. This is not good for anyone's writing development. While it can be tempting to think that the child's language learning is bringing her and other students around her down, that is simply not the case. All students have different things that are their primary learning focus, and they will need to rely on the community to help meet those goals. Additionally, they will need us to be guides in that work so that these supports are seen as a positive temporary support.

Another thing to consider when forming triads is that they will need us to teach into them. One helpful strategy is to guide the student with a more beginning level of English to participate first in their dominant language, then in English. That habit allows practice in two languages for both the speaker and the listener. The time it takes students to orally produce language varies greatly, especially in the upper grades, where children often don't want to be seen as different. That initial oral language production can take weeks, even months, before it shows up in an academic setting. When students are encouraged to share in a supportive and predictable environment there is more possibility for growth.

Additionally you will likely want to offer a variety of nonhuman tools and resources for writing. You'll no doubt want to be aware of which tools your students choose and notice if or when they may be too reliant on particular tools. In between conferences or small groups, investigate what students use on their own and if it is helping or complicating their writing time. The need to be "right" can often overpower the chances we hope writers will take and slow their language and writing growth. A few tools you might consider include:

- Access to dictionaries for English and their dominant language, preferably picture as well as word only. A few of my favorites include: *My First Spanish-English Picture Dictionary* from Publications International, any of the *Oxford Picture Dictionary* series (which range in languages from Urdu to Chinese), the classic *Webster's* (which does not include pictures), and my new favorite, the *Milet Mini-Picture Dictionary* series from Milet Publishing—these cover a huge range of languages in a beautiful, portable package.

- Plain white paper, or paper with room for pictures so that sketching and labeling can be used as part of rehearsal. It is crucial that if these paper choices are offered, they are modeled as valid types of paper to use in the classroom, and not just "special" paper for certain kids.

- Picture files with common words illustrated with images. Students can use these to find words that are tricky to find in the dictionary, but they can also be used to help with cultural knowledge, and even inspiration for possible writing topics.

- Sentence stems on chart paper, or better yet, index cards that can be kept at the student's fingertips. These sentence stems can change as the unit changes. *One day . . . In this essay I will show . . . For example . . . Some people think* _____, *but I think* _____. (See Figure 4–4: Sentence Stems by Type.)

- A tablet or laptop that allows the student to use translation software, picture libraries, and to quickly search online for needed words and phrases. Two common and popular apps include iTranslate and Google Translate.

Now, clearly there will be direct teaching to support your English language learners. When teaching English language learners, just as with every other learner, there should be a combination of whole-class, small-group, and one-on-one sessions. When teaching in a whole-class setting, many teachers I know aim to keep their teaching as streamlined as possible. Which means keeping the lesson as short as possible, including a lot of modeling and

Figure 4–4 Sentence Stems by Type

Type	Sentence Stems
Narrative	• One day . . . • After that . . . • The next day . . . • _____ wanted _____ but _____ • _____ felt • _____ said, "_____" • All of a sudden . . . • Finally,
Opinion/Argument	• I believe . . . • I think this because . . . • In this essay I will show . . . • One reason . . . • Another reason . . . • For example . . . • This shows . . . • In conclusion . . .
Informational	• There are _____ facts to know about _____. • One surprising fact is _____. • Research shows that _____. • _____ connects with _____ because _____.

visuals and using a lot of repeated language. By keeping lessons short, we ensure that students are not spending most of their class time passively being talked at, but rather spending their time exploring and engaging in language use. Many teachers who work with the Reading and Writing Project like to use the same phrases for different parts of their lessons every day so that students are more easily able to focus on the new content. Phrases such as: *Today I'm going to teach you . . . , Watch me as I write . . . , Did you notice how I . . . , Now it's your turn to try . . . , When you go off to write today . . .* all become cues for the learner, and the consistency they offer allows for deeper understanding because their predictability allows students to focus on the new. If for whatever reason streamlining a particular lesson is tricky, you could also consider preteaching the lesson, or at least the vocabulary that will likely be new for the student. Some teachers also find including an extra opportunity for students to be actively involved in the lesson, as well as repeating the teaching point many times in the same words, can help students get their grappling hooks around important strategies and ideas.

Of course, one of the beauties of teaching writing is that it is built-in language instruction. Students are learning how to develop and express their ideas in the written language. For many students, especially ones who are not fond of speaking, writing offers a less risky way to practice language. Because of that, wise teachers use the fact that every writing lesson can be a language lesson as well by calling out explicitly what the students are learning as writers and about English in general. For example, a teacher doing work on transitions might say, "Writers, one of the things we do for our readers is make sure all the pieces of our writing fit smoothly together. We call these words transitions. There are a handful of words that writers regularly use to make transitions. A few are . . ." Some teachers go as far as to mark up their lesson plans with a writing teaching point and a language teaching point for every whole-class lesson. A teacher might have a minilesson written like this in her lesson plan book:

- Writing strategy: Writers can think of places as a way to inspire possible story ideas.

- Language lesson: Names for common settings, and words associated with them. Examples: school (desk, chair, books, teacher, lunch, homework, students), playground (swings, slide, monkey bars, run, play, friends), home (family, table, chairs, television, bed, kitchen, bathroom)

Just like when learning a new skill like sea kayaking or figuring out your new mobile phone, the more often you try something and return to it repeatedly the more likely you are to learn it and have it become a part of you. Consider exposing students to grammatical concepts and language objectives repeatedly across days and across weeks. They are more apt to bring it into their own language if it is something they have experienced numerous times as the meaning grows.

Of course, while whole-class instruction is crucial to give students access to the grade-appropriate curriculum, it is also just as important, if not more so, to make sure that we are teaching students what they need. For that reason, we will want to make sure that our students learning English are being regularly met with in small groups and one-on-one conferences. When distinguishing between when to work with a student one-on-one and when to pull a small group, you will want to consider both the number of students who need the teaching and the method you plan to use. So, for example, if you have two students who both need help building longer and more complex sentences, and you want them to practice that sentence-building work in writing and in spoken word, you might work with them as a partnership in a very small group. If, however, you have one student who has more language experience than another student and while they are both working on story language, one is working primarily on labeling objects and the other is working on verb phrases, you will want to work with them one-on-one. Even though it might be tempting to put them together because they are both learning English and share a dominant language, in this instance, because your teaching objectives are so different, it will be better to teach them separately, knowing that there will be other times when it will make more sense for them to be grouped together.

When considering other kinds of grouping, for small groups of around two to four kids, some teachers decide to group students based on the level of language acquisition they are currently at. Others like to mix things up so that students are better able to have cross-group conversation. You might encourage learners to have those cards with language prompts you created together to give them support as they participate in conversation. You might choose to do a mix of things. No matter what you decide, what is important is that the small-group instruction is tailored to the needs of the students in the group and that they have a lot of opportunity within that group to practice the strategy being taught in the company of others.

Finally, depending on the level of English language acquisition students are currently at, many teachers opt to winnow down the number of lessons within any one writing unit to the bare bones. In other words, if the original planned unit called for teaching three strategies for collecting possible ideas, another four strategies for rehearsing and developing, three strategies for drafting, seven for revising, and three for editing, equaling about twenty teaching points, the teacher might opt to cut those down to just what is most important as in Figure 4–5. In other words, twenty sessions might become ten to twelve, with some lessons that seem particularly important retaught and other lessons that seem more repertoire-like being used for conferences and small-group work. In this way, a teacher can attack a skill a couple of different ways, but use the same language lessons, and offer more time for the student who needs to manually grab every word that she uses.

Figure 4–5
Unit Reconsidered

Unit One - Personal Narrative

Lessons: 1 - Think of people that matter and moments connected to them

2 - Think of times of strong emotion

3 - Think of turning point memories

} collecting

4 - Choose story idea & practice it through storytelling

5 - Plan using a timeline

6 - Try 3 different leads action, setting or dialogue

} rehearsing

7 - Draft by re-living moment

8 - Revise by developing most important parts of story

9 - Use character actions to show feelings

10 - Describe setting to mirror character internal life

- Revise ending for meaning

} drafting & revising

11 - Revise for precise words

12 - Revise for end points

13 - Edit for end points

14 - Edit for spelling

15 - Edit for quotation marks

} editing

✳ Ongoing Work: Finding Authentic Reasons for Language Practice and Mastery

As I mentioned earlier in this chapter, deciding to embrace teaching students who are learning English is not something that will be tackled and checked off the list by the end of the month. Or even the end of the year. Because of new research, a new global society, and the new expectations constantly incorporated into our practice, this will be an ongoing struggle and adventure. One of the best ways to be sure that you are always ahead of the curve is to give students endless opportunities to practice speaking and writing in their dominant language (if they can) as well as their new language. This means you will want to set aside time each day for this practice.

Cheryl Tyler, when she was principal of P.S. 277 in the Bronx, used to encourage her teachers to begin each day with hot-topic conversations in order to build a curriculum of talk. Teachers would choose topics that they knew were irresistible to the students (the World Series, school uniforms, neighborhood issues) and have students practice speaking about the topic for a few days, then ending the week writing a short piece based on the repeatedly practiced conversations.

The more functional and purposeful the task is, the more likely students will want to take risks in order to engage. Students can create signs for their classroom and their school building. They might write book reviews and field trip directions. They can craft bilingual picture books for their reading buddies in the younger grades. I know teachers who host bagel breakfasts, math congresses, and speech competitions regularly, all in the name of making talk and language practice a regular, predictable part of the school day. The most successful teachers always take time to make sure English is not the only language being learned and discussed. In another interesting use for seminars, some teachers encourage students to teach seminars on common vocabulary and phrases in their dominant language to other students, allowing the English language learner to be the expert, as well as opening up another line of communication.

The strongest schools don't stop at the school day. At Hope Street School in Los Angeles, families are invited to school-based workshops in order to learn strategies for reading aloud to their children, improving their own English, and communicating with their children's teachers. At East Side Middle School in Manhattan, the principal, Mark Federman, encourages parents to watch television with the closed captions on, alongside their children. This allows not only language reinforcement via the written word, but also opportunities for families to practice language through conversations about the shows they are watching.

Much of what I've described in this chapter will get you and your students started on a great writing year. However, it does not account for many intricacies of English language learning, including specific vocabulary instruction, use of idioms, etc. The field of educating additional language learners is one that begs for regular study and refreshing. I highly recommend that you do some professional reading or attend professional development dedicated to this topic. A few of the strongest voices in the field (voices that dovetail well with writing workshop) include:

- Christina Celic, author of *English Language Learners Day by Day*
- Ofelia Garcia, author of *Educating Emergent Bilinguals*
- Pauline Gibbons, author of *Scaffolding Language, Scaffolding Learning*
- Mary Cappellini, author of *Balancing Reading and Language Learning*
- David Freeman and Yvonne Freeman, authors of *English Language Learners: The Essential Guide*
- Ruth Swinney and Patricia Velasco, authors of *Connecting Content and Academic Language for English Language Learners and Struggling Students*

If you aren't already familiar with their work, you will likely want to seek out their books and workshops to add to your growing knowledge base.

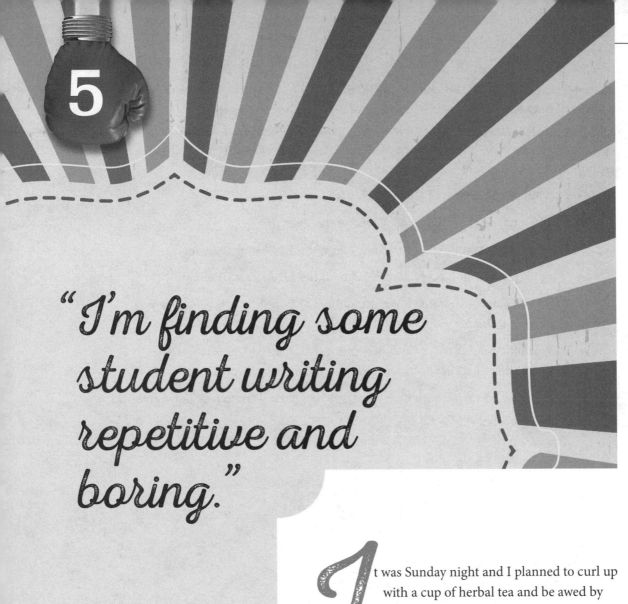

5

"I'm finding some student writing repetitive and boring."

It was Sunday night and I planned to curl up with a cup of herbal tea and be awed by my students' latest drafted writing pieces. The first one I picked up was about a trip to an amusement park nearby. The next one was about a roller coaster. The next one was about a soccer game. I switched to coffee.

The one after that was about a basketball game. The next three were about pet dogs. By the time I was done wading through the writing, I noticed that most of the writing was either about sports, amusement parks, or pets. There were occasional flashes of color in the gray sameness of their writing, but for the most part, there was nothing to differentiate one piece of writing from the next other than the name written on the top of the page. I was bored to tears and somehow had to return to school the next day with enough energy to get them fired up about revising their writing. Normally I would tell them how exciting the pieces were and how I couldn't wait to see how much more they could do. But now, I felt as if anything I said about most of the pieces would be a lie.

It's one of the dirty little secrets of teaching writing. Sometimes it can feel boring. Sometimes hearing about kids' lives and the things they want to tell us can leave us stifling yawns. It has led more than one kindhearted teacher to give up on the whole enterprise of giving students topic choice. "Maybe if I assign them fascinating topics the writing will get more interesting," the reasoning goes. But unfortunately, it rarely ends up working out that way. Student topic choice is still paramount for writing workshop to be successful, but there are definitely times that hopping ourselves up on double shots of espresso when it's time to read their writing sounds like the best way to go.

✳ What Stops Us: We Confuse the Writing with the Writer

For those of us who are dyed-in-the-wool writing workshop teachers, the first time we fell in love with the method was usually the first time we heard an exquisite piece of student writing. I distinctly remember sitting in an auditorium filled with fellow teachers when I heard Lucy Calkins read a piece by a girl named Marisol who had never had a birthday party. I cried real tears over both the tragedy that was Marisol's life and the fact that her teacher was able to give her an outlet for those stories through her writing. Writing workshop is meant to give students a voice to tell their stories, their ideas, their passions. When writing workshop is going well we uncover amazing quirks, laugh-out-loud adventures, and tear-jerking experiences. It is the best stuff about being a teacher.

So it feels particularly disappointing when students are not writing meaningful pieces. When they seem to all be writing on the surface level. The writing may be fine. It could pass any rubric you put before it, but it just doesn't have the pizzazz we hunger to see. Sometimes it's because the students merely opted to cling too closely to the teacher demonstration. If the teacher wrote about her lost dog, several students will write about their lost dogs (or cats, or hamsters).

Sometimes the writing is boring because it appears to have no heart, no real depth. Yes, it's a story about how a student scored a goal at the soccer game, but there's no indication that this goal matters for anyone — not the writer, not the team, not even the kid's family. Or it's an essay about something that seems like it should be juicy — people shouldn't smoke.

But it's so full of hearsay and lackluster information that smoking almost begins to sound like a great option.

No matter what the reason we find it boring, what really makes that challenging is that we desperately do not want the writing to be boring. Not just because we have to use our precious free time to grade it, but for many of us, writing workshop is the highlight of our day. We live for those funny stories and piercing ideas. We want to hear students' authentic voices. And when the writing veers into monotony we start to worry that perhaps either we are getting bored with our students, or else our students just really have nothing to say. I have heard more than one exasperated teacher say to me, "They clearly can't do writing workshop. They don't do anything worth writing about." Of course, no one really wants to think that. We all know that some of the best writing is about the most mundane things: a vignette about washing dishes with Mom, an essay about arguing with a big brother, a guide to changing diapers. And that is precisely what makes this so tough—because we do not want to be bored by our students or think less of their lives. We might even feel a bit guilty for that second shot of espresso after reading the dead goldfish story.

✳ See Opportunity: Help Students Push for Personal Meaning-Making

It would be very easy to just throw up your hands and say, "Eh, some writing is just going to be boring. I'm not going to get too upset about it." But, I want to argue, at the center of a strong writing workshop, one that works for teachers and kids, is topic choice—the ability for the writer to chart her own course and decide which things are worthy of writing about. If you believe that, as I do, you definitely do not want to quit.

Another reason it's important that we help our students move past safe and boring writing is a selfish one. Good writing gives writing teachers energy. Right now, more than any other time in recent memory, teaching has become a slog for many people. The amount of pressure, the scrutiny, the high-stakes nature of our work, can make it difficult to rally. When we hold a piece of student writing that gives us a window into a child's life or thoughts, we are reminded why we do what we do. Helping our students reach their writing potential will also help us reach our teaching potential.

Communities are built by the risks the members of those communities take. When you think about your closest friend, or perhaps your spouse, there is usually a moment when you went from being fond of each other to incredibly close. Usually that moment has to do with a connection of some kind. Perhaps a shared experience, or perhaps a confessed secret or shared story. Classroom communities are not different. When teachers and students decide to share pieces of their lives together, they risk embarrassment, misunderstanding, or worse, humiliation. But, if those things don't transpire, there are no new connections formed, no new understandings, no new bridges.

Perhaps most importantly, students do have important things to share in their writing. Maybe not things that will change the course of world events, but things that are important in the life of a child. The death of a carefully tended tadpole, watching a father cry, helping a baby sister learn to walk, admiring a grandparent, can all be explored and shared through writing workshop. Unfortunately a lot of people, our students included, don't really think their lives are worth writing about. They think only people who go on exotic trips or stand on stages have writerly lives. We need to show students how to value the small and mundane, the common and the strange, as wonderful material for writing. When they see that, this often spins off into them seeing their own lives as having more value.

Often though, students don't know exactly what they are trying to say. They just pick a topic and go with it because it feels comfortable or it's something that they feel a need to write about for some reason. In those instances, students need us to help them find what matters in the topics that they choose. When they find a willing and expert audience for their writing, they will be able to have the coaching they need to turn it into something worthy of them.

✳ Experiment: Invite Risk Taking and Believe in the Writer's Intent

One of the easiest ways to invite risk-taking and help support more lively and unique writing is to choose mentor texts that are not only good examples of the type of writing you are teaching, but also are beautiful, jarring, unusual, or inspiring. It's tempting to stick to mentor texts that tell stories we've already heard, that share ideas we already agree with, that teach about topics that are very run-of-the-mill. They technically get the job done. Students see examples of how writing in this genre can go.

However, if you notice that your students' writing falls in line with that same vanilla writing, you might want to kick things up a notch. Consider choosing mentor texts for narrative writing where the characters make bad choices, do strange things, or don't end well, such as "Everything Will Be Okay" by James Howe, "Shortcut" by Donald Cruise, "Visiting Day" by Jacqueline Woodson, or "Thirteen and a Half" by Rachel Vail. Explore persuasive writing where the author chooses an unpopular side of an argument such as *I Am a Booger . . . Treat Me with Respect* by Julia Cook or *Animals Nobody Loves* by Seymour Simon. Offer informational texts about things that are either fascinating, familiar, or both, such as *Naked Mole Rats* by Kristin Petrie, *Farts in the Wild: A Spotter's Guide* by H. W. Smeldit or *No Monkeys, No Chocolate* by Melissa Stewart.

Another way to help spice up your students' writing is to shine a spotlight on any student who is taking risks, or is dipping their toe into risk, or looks like they might be considering dipping their toe into something interesting. When we make a child famous for doing something, or getting close to doing something we want the rest of the class to try, we go a long way toward making this option more enticing to others. Kids love to get attention for doing good work, and they also like to try things that others do so that they can bask in the overflow glow. This might look something like this: "Everybody, Maggie did something so amazing today. I just want everyone to hear about it. Maggie was between two ideas for her personal narrative. One was about a time that she got ice cream with her best friend. It's a fun story. They laugh; they eat too much. Then they go home. She had another story idea. In this one she pushed her brother off the front porch. It's not a flattering story, but in it there's a lot of action. And it's one that is unique to Maggie. Only she can tell it. I'm wondering if anyone has stories like Maggie does that you're thinking about. Like ones only you can tell." Then I might ask students to turn and talk to their partners and review their story options, holding in their mind the decisions that Maggie made.

Another powerful option, albeit a more personally risky one because it puts you, the teacher, more on stage, is to up the ante for your modeled writing. For a couple of years I used the same story about riding the Cyclone at Coney Island with my friend. It was a well-written story, but it was also sort of blah. And it led students to think that good writing didn't require much heart. I had the amazing serendipity to hear Donald Graves speak while I was wrestling with this issue. He spoke about the importance of writing in front of and beside our students. He suggested that rather than trying to oversimplify and sanitize our adult lives, we should instead write about the time in our lives when we were the same age as our students. So, if we teach fifth-graders, we should endeavor to remember our fifth-grade selves and write about those stories, ideas, and interests. For example, in fifth-grade, my best friend and I got in trouble because instead of clapping the chalkboard erasers clean we pounded them on the asphalt. Our fifth-grade teacher made us use rags and water to clean up the mess. I was also passionately against littering and loved to learn as much as I could about hypnosis. All of these are great topics to bring into a classroom.

There are certainly a couple of tricky things for this. What if your writing is framed from an adult's perspective? What if you can't really remember your ten-year-old or eight-year-old self? What if your writing gets too interesting and the kids lose sight of the teaching? I recommend you make a mini-project and revive those memories, while reconnecting with your child-self and child perspective. A couple of things you might do to get back in touch with your younger self:

Find pictures of yourself at that age. I get one look at that royal blue v neck top and I am back in the 80s.

Listen to music that was popular at the time. If I go anywhere a Diana Ross song is playing, I am suddenly a Girl Scout again.

Eat candy and other food that was popular at the time. Nothing brings back memories to me quite like Big League Chew and Fun Dip.

Follow your nose. Brain research tells us that one of the quickest paths to memory is to smell something connected to a time period. Folger's coffee, bacon, orange blossoms, wet dog, will all take me back in time almost as effectively as a time machine.

Sketch a map of your childhood haunts (childhood neighborhood, school, camp), annotating it with moments that stand out. I am surprised, no matter how many times I do this activity, how many new memories I uncover.

Consider current issues, passions, struggles, and remember a related experience or idea from childhood. For example, recently I was grappling with the idea that my parents were getting older and their mortality. And it started to make me think about possible losses in my life. Of course, that's not a conversation I would get into with students. But I could think about losses when I was their age, like when my favorite teacher left on maternity leave, or my best friend told me she was transferring to a new school.

Once you have a few memories at your disposal you should be ready to go. Those memories will not only be good fodder for narratives, but will also likely remind you of some of your strong childhood opinions and interests. Students will understand that the things you are sharing are actually meaningful to you and uniquely your experiences. This will likely compel them to share their own more readily — which of course leads to better writing. Another plus of this strategy is that you can mine this material for years to come.

The last suggestion I would make is probably the toughest, most risky, and also the most rewarding. And, I suppose in a way, it is intrinsically behind all the other strategies mentioned, even if it isn't always explicitly said. It requires a leap of faith. It's something I learned directly from Lucy Calkins, which is that we need to believe that students do have something important to say and they need us to help them get at it. When we read the sort of dull and generic story about getting a new puppy, we need to act bowled over. We should say, "Wow! Look at this writing. It feels so big to me." And it's in the act of believing in the author's intent and prodding the writer to talk more about his intent, always leaving room for the young writer to draw her own conclusions about significance, that many writers find their way to their own truth—a truth they sometimes felt but didn't *know*. We need to do this even if we have some doubts and aren't entirely convinced there is something more meaningful there.

There's a story I've told before about how this experience, of taking what I've learned directly from Lucy, made a huge impact on me and the teachers I was working with, and of course a certain student (although, perhaps less so him). It was my first year working as a staff developer at the Reading and Writing Project and I was working with a group of sixth-grade teachers in Connecticut. The students were studying personal essay and the teachers were talking about how there were students whose topics were just sort of boring, felt almost shallow. After we were done with the day's minilesson, I asked the teacher whose classroom we were doing our lab site in to indicate a student who was falling into that pattern. She pointed to a nondescript boy writing quietly at his desk. I pulled up a chair next to him and the teachers gathered around in a semicircle to listen in.

"What are you working on Robert?" I asked.

He pointed to the stack of papers and folders in front of me. "My personal essay."

"Tell me about it," I said, poising my pen to show Robert I was getting ready to capture anything he had to say.

"My thesis is 'Christmas is my favorite holiday,'" he said, his face not showing any sort of emotion. A few of the teachers exchanged glances.

I took a deep breath and remembered that I had to believe. "Wow. That sounds like something really important to you. That is . . . wow." I smiled a lot and nodded.

Robert looked at me and said, "Well, actually, it really is important to me. I really, really, love Christmas." He was smiling now. A shy smile, but a smile nonetheless.

"Well, don't leave me hanging here, tell me more about what you're doing," I asked.

He spread his papers out across his desk as he spoke. "I have different reasons Christmas is my favorite holiday. One is that it's my favorite holiday because I eat a lot of food. Another reason is because I get presents. And the third reason is because we watch videos."

The teachers started to exchange more meaningful glances. I was starting to sweat a bit, but I didn't show that to Robert. I acted absolutely enthralled. "That sounds incredibly important. All of those things." Robert nodded. "If you were to point to just one of those things that seems more important than anything else, which one would it be?"

Robert stacked up his papers. I was truthfully hoping he would say food. I knew there were a lot of things we could work on with food. Even presents would be okay. We could be thinking about motivation and stories behind the presents. But no matter what, I was really hoping he wouldn't say videos. I knew that would be a tough hole to dig out of.

"Videos," Robert said, beaming. "My favorite part of Christmas is definitely the videos."

My heart sank. I could feel the tension from the teachers. They were actually feeling a bit for me, knowing this was a tough turn. But, I took a deep breath, nodded with as much enthusiasm as I could muster. I had to believe. "Oh wow. Videos. That is just so important, isn't it?" I said. "I mean, there is just so much in there, so much to say about videos on Christmas. I would really love to hear what you have to say about them." I leaned forward, as excitedly as I could.

Robert was sitting toward me now, leaning his body forward, his pen clutched, a small smile on his lips. He lowered his voice a bit as if to tell a public secret. "Yeah. They are so important," he said. "Every year, after we've opened the presents and eaten all the food, my whole family climbs onto the couch to watch videos together." I nodded. "We record every Christmas. Then we watch all the Christmases we've had together on Christmas. And since my Dad died, Christmas is the only time I get to see him. My mom can't stand to watch all the videos at any other time. But on Christmas, she lets us watch them, and it's like we're all together again."

I won't lie. My eyes filled with tears. So did the rest of the teachers. I tried to keep my voice steady as I said, "That feels very important to me. Maybe that's what your essay is really about?"

Robert nodded. He didn't even wait for me to leave. He was already bringing new paper to start a new draft where his thesis would revolve around his father.

Here's the thing: Robert had nothing in his original draft about his father. His reasons and evidence list all the foods his family ate and all the presents they would get. The section on video watching just talks about snuggling on the couch with popcorn watching home movies. It never once mentions Robert's dad. And clearly that's not because Robert wasn't thinking about him.

I don't know exactly why it works this way, but my hunch is that kids, and some adult writers, have a subconscious need to write about particular topics, but they don't consciously know why. Most amateur writers, kid or adult, tend to think that they have nothing very important to say. But, when they are faced with someone they trust and who believes in them, they often begin to believe in themselves and start to see ways in which their writing might be obscuring deeper truths. As their teachers, we just need to have a lot of faith, some acting chops, and the patience to listen to them and keep repeating, "That's so important, tell me more," as they slowly make their way into meaning.

One last little tip — not everything we help students uncover will feel meaningful to us. Sometimes, all we will help them find out is just how funny the boogers were or why Minecraft is the best game ever. But, if that is what is meaningful to them and unique to them, I can at least assure you it will be less boring for you and a whole lot more purposeful for them. It is also helpful (and hopeful) to keep in mind that many, many professional writers cover the same writing terrain over and over again, each time uncovering a new layer. Some professional writers spend a lifetime doing it. So, it is entirely possible that the more your writers do that same circling back, they might also uncover layers, maybe not getting to the kernel they are after for years after they have left your classroom.

✳ Ongoing Work: Maintaining the Conditions for Risk Taking

Fast forward a few months. You've brought the edgiest mentor texts you could find. You've dug deep into your own past. You even have a risky-writers share session on Fridays for writers who've gone out on a limb. You have listened and believed until you thought Tinkerbell was going to fly. And then you sit down with a stack of recently published student pieces and find yourself rubbing your eyes and getting up to make a fresh pot of coffee.

I would suggest first that you make sure you tried most of the things I suggested. If, upon reflection, you realize that you are missing something, that might be the puzzle piece your students need. If you instead realize that, nope, you did everything, exactly as described, then you might want to have a heart-to-heart talk with your writers. If it's the whole class, then bring the whole class into the meeting area. If it's a small group of kids, pull them aside someday during writing workshop. And just be as transparent, in a nonhurtful way, as possible. You might say that you notice that some of their pieces seem to almost always be about similar topics to yours and to other writers. You might say that the pieces feel like they lack the energy you know these students have for the interests in their lives. Tell them you're puzzled. Ask them if they'd like to launch an inquiry with you as to how to make their writing more closely align with the individual people they are and what matters most to them. This may or may not lead to a discussion right away. If it does, feel free to let it run. If not, simply let the students know that you will reconvene this group to discuss their findings in a set amount of time. Often in the act of exploring an inquiry the writers will find what they need.

Now, just to be clear—this kind of conversation is probably the riskiest thing discussed in this chapter, because, as I'm sure you can well imagine, students' feelings could get hurt and they could very well shut down and retreat even further. In order to help ensure that does not happen, you might want to keep a few guidelines in mind:

- *Own as much of the problem as you can.* "I feel like there's something I'm not explaining enough or giving you enough examples of," rather than, "Your writing is just so shallow and uninteresting. What is going on with you?"

- *Share examples of student writing of the sort you are hoping for.* Sometimes students aren't doing this kind of writing because they have not seen enough samples from their peers, particularly with their teacher as curator, explaining exactly what makes this type of writing worthwhile.

- *Ask about places they feel free to take risks and consider with them ways to bring that atmosphere into writing workshop.* Sometimes when students think about math class or art they realize that there are places in the school day that they take risks.

- *Try to do more listening than talking.* Sometimes this might mean using some serious wait time, and encouraging students to talk with a partner before talking to the whole group, but as much as possible, students need to take the lead in this discussion.

- *Be prepared to find out whatever there is to find out.* It might be that one time you said something that students felt was harsh. Perhaps there is some quiet mockery that happens among the students when you aren't looking. Maybe the kids are intimidated because you are such a great writer. No matter what they say, be prepared to handle it with grace.

- *It is okay to return to the conversation at a later date.* Sometimes in tough conversations like this, issues can come up that need some reflection, or else it ends up that nothing comes up and we need to regroup. Assume that if you are sitting down to have this conversation with your students, it will likely be part of a series of conversations.

- *Accept that people have different definitions of meaningful.* Humor is very important to many people. Certain topics hold some people in rapt attention, while confusing others. Some people can not resist ickiness. Knowing this can help us understand that not every child will write about a topic that feels meaningful to us. But, it will in fact be chock full of meaning for them.

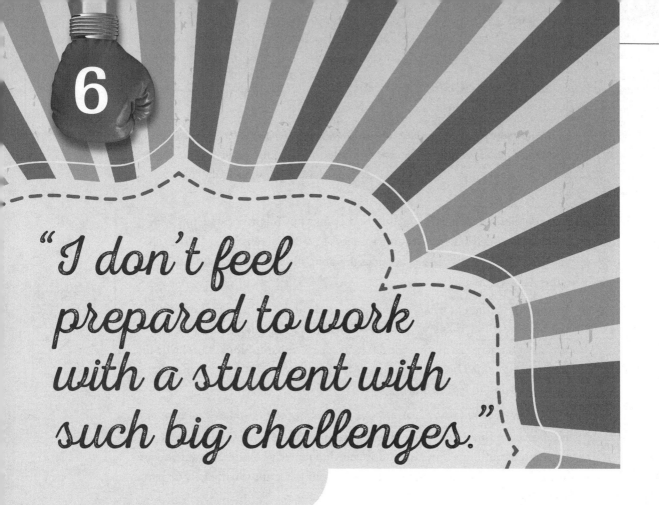

6

"I don't feel prepared to work with a student with such big challenges."

Several years ago I felt like I needed a change in my teaching, so I spoke to my principal about possibilities. Maybe I should change grades? Maybe I should consider going for a new license? My principal asked if I would consider co-teaching in an inclusive classroom with another teacher. A percentage of my students would have Individualized Education Plans (IEPs) and a larger percentage would be part of the general education population. My initial instinct was excitement. I loved the idea of co-teaching. I also was always a fan of having diverse learners and knew in this setup I would have the most diverse class I had ever had. But as I considered the idea I started to get nervous. What did I really know about working with students who had special needs? What if I screwed them up somehow?

I was on the edge of backing out when Jen, the teacher I planned to co-teach with, said "Colleen, you know what to do. You've had students with IEPs your whole career. You've also taught students who had other challenges, which had not been identified. But you will figure it out. There's no magic bullet. You just need to teach them."

Based on conversations I've had with other educators since, I don't think I'm alone in having those feelings. Perhaps you're not considering making the switch from a general education to a special education setting, but do have students in your class with IEPs or severe writing challenges who are not receiving formal services. It can be challenging to know what to do.

✳ What Stops Us: We Might Not Get Students as Far as We Want Them to Go

The good and bad news about working with students with writing challenges is that, unlike many of the other struggles in this book, most of our colleagues, or even just people we know, acknowledge that it can be hard work to move a student who has learning needs, whether or not we have been formally trained to work with those students specifically. While I could imagine creating a very long list of what makes it hard, I decided that most of the things that would be on that list seem to break down into five categories:

- *Battling misconceptions.* When working with students with learning challenges, misconceptions abound. They come from class parents. They come from other students. They come from us. There are many misunderstandings and confusions around students who struggle academically, whether they have been identified as having a disability or not. Some of us have hang-ups about certain disabilities. Some students worry that it might be contagious. There's a habit of blaming the learner when people don't understand that learning and production are often inconsistent. Often, getting over the hurdle of those misconceptions and opening our own and others' minds are the hardest things for us to overcome.

- *Feeling afraid to make mistakes.* This was my biggest concern. What if I somehow taught the wrong thing or the wrong way and messed up a student's learning? I hadn't had specialized training in the needs all my students had (physical disabilities, emotional dysfunctions, neurological disorders). How could I possibly know what the right thing to do was at any given moment? So much of my teaching was instinctive — was it okay to still be instinctive? I think for many teachers, students with significant challenges with learning feel more vulnerable. Knowing that fear is normal was helpful for me.

- *Knowing the right level of support to give students.* There is a balancing act with any student — how much struggle is good for learning? How much leads to frustration? How much makes a student dependent? How much empowers? Making those decisions on a daily, sometimes minute-by-minute basis can be daunting. Knowing what supports are appropriate for which situation or need can also be tricky.

- *Worries about particular struggles or diagnosis.* This is where it's important to be honest. We all have areas of comfort. We also have areas where we feel less comfortable. I've had friends in my life with Down syndrome, so I am very comfortable working with kids who have Down syndrome. However, I have less experience with children who have hallucinations. So, when one of my students was diagnosed as having schizophrenia, I was more than a little nervous about how I would support that student, as well as how my actions might affect the rest of the classroom.

- *When there's no diagnosis but you know something is wrong.* Some students will have families that, for a variety of reasons, will not have their child evaluated. Other students are evaluated, but the things the student is struggling with do not point the way to one clear diagnosis. For some of us, this is the hardest challenge. With information in hand, we feel as if we would be so much more likely to be successful with this student. Having to go almost completely with our instincts, with little or no support from an outside source, can be frustrating and daunting.

✳ See Opportunity: Value Diversity of Student Assets and Growth

While all of the above obstacles can definitely make teaching students with significant writing issues challenging, there are also many opportunities in working with these students. First and foremost, as always, is the opportunity to reflect and refine our teaching in ways we might not have done otherwise. One realization that many teachers have shared with me is that *there's no one right way to do things*. Realizing this is a great weight off the shoulders of those of us who hate to mess things up for kids. Strong teachers will try out many things with their students, *all* of their students. Some of those things will work like magic.

Others won't. The thing many of us learn who work with students with significant struggles is that there isn't a cool strategy chart somewhere that we can refer to that says, "Needs fine motor support—then needs to use Special Pen X." What trained specialists will tell you is that, while it's nice to know these things, Special Pen X doesn't always work. So, the best choice for teachers who are trying to meet the diverse needs of their learners is to just try things that seem to make sense and sound like they would work. Trial and error is our friend.

When faced fairly regularly (daily, or hourly, or in some cases minute by minute) with things we don't know about, we could look at this as pointing out our deficiencies, or we could decide to embrace this great opportunity to learn. The best teachers, as we all know, are the ones who never stop learning. That said, for those of us who are in the profession for a while, we sometimes need to look more and more for those opportunities to stretch ourselves. If we decide to undertake the challenge of embracing our work with students with significant learning challenges, we will have built-in chances to outgrow our own best work on a daily basis.

Another opportunity that working with students with diverse learning needs gives us is the opportunity to look more closely at the term "disability" and define it for our students and ourselves. To be clear (not that this will surprise you), I have never been fond of terms around disability that try to turn it into a positive thing—like "handi-capable." When I was fifteen years old, I was diagnosed with a physical disability. I remember feeling both relieved (I wasn't crazy—there *is* something wrong with me) and deeply embarrassed (oh no—there *is* something wrong with me). Part of me was thrilled to be given alternative options to gym class. I hated that my mother had to sign a form saying I didn't require a special bus. The term "disability" then, and now, has come to mean for me that there is something that other "typical" people can do that the disabled person cannot do—at least not with some supports. I have also come to believe that all of us have some sort of disability, some sort of way we are in the world, a thing we can't do that other people can. This doesn't make us better or worse than anyone else. However, it does mean that most of us experience struggle in some way. By reflecting on my own disabilities—obvious and not—I become a more patient and empathetic person and teacher. When I am working with a student who has a disability, I can't always assume they feel negative about the way they live in the world. I have friends who embrace their atypical nature. But, the opportunity I am given is a chance to reflect on difference, seen and unseen, in the way all humans, including myself, interact with the world.

Also important to consider is, if you have been paying attention to the trends in education lately, you know one of the bigger trends is to move more and more children out of self-contained special education settings into general education settings with supports.

This is happening for a variety of reasons, not the least of which is the passing of IDEA, which requires that students be placed in the least restrictive environment. This is also due to the unfortunate fact that a disportionate number of students who are classified as being in need of special education services and settings are male children of color, and many people have rallied to try to make this less likely to happen. By and large, many people believe that this move of more students moving from special education classrooms to general education classrooms with supports is a better choice for most students in need of services.

Consequently, as more students are placed in least restrictive environments we will encounter more diverse learning needs. Ideally, as educators, we will all welcome the opportunity to have classroom communities that more closely mirror society. We know that on average, 17 percent of the general populace has a disability of some sort. We also know that laws and public opinions around educational inclusivity are changing. This is an amazing opportunity to be on the ground floor of a child's development as both a learner and a member of society.

Another one of the opportunities presented by working with students with diverse learning needs is that the more difference we experience, the more we are prepared for. When I was worried about working with a student who was diagnosed as having schizophrenia, I wasn't thinking about how much I would learn. Now I know that after having worked with a student whose needs are new to me, I will have gained a new set of strategies and tools. Additionally, actually having a diagnosis, while daunting at first, also gives me a ton of information that I did not have before. My student who was diagnosed as having schizophrenia was a student I had taught for months, knowing she needed something different, but not being sure what needs I should be prioritizing. With the diagnosis, I actually had a clearer sense of focus as I worked with her.

Finally, and this is perhaps a bit of a selfish thing to say, because it can feed our egos, but students who have writing challenges are often the biggest success stories. There are many things I love about teaching writing. I love that students have a platform for sharing their stories. I love that because of writing process students have a chance to "do-over" in a way we never really get in life. I also love that writing is thinking made visible—capturing it on the page—and therefore capturing growth over time. For all these reasons, when students are challenged by writing we actually get to see the struggle on the page—and the growth made visible. And unlike something like riding a bike where first you do it, then you wobble, then you have it, we (the students and teachers) get to see this growth incrementally. Additionally, because writing is so widespread across the curriculum and has so many high stakes and personally important uses for students, when students improve it has a ripple effect across their learning and across their person.

✳ Experiment: Become a Collaborative Researcher

Let me start by suggesting that you try to be optimistic . . . a little bit. Don't worry, you didn't just somehow slip through a wormhole and land in another book. I am still very much a pessimist about almost everything. Except for kids. I fundamentally believe in *their* capacity for positivity, for growth and change. And, I believe strongly that if we are to move students, especially ones who struggle the most fiercely, we need to believe in their innate ability to learn. I recently heard Kylene Beers talk about how she wished that when every teacher spoke about what a student struggled with they added the word *yet*. "She doesn't write with structure . . . yet." "He is not able to spell conventionally . . . yet." The *yet* brings that hopeful-ness and expectation right into the picture so that any deficit we might be seeing we see as only temporary.

As part of this, naturally, one of the first things we want to do is make sure that the student knows we care about him for being him. Not because of or in spite of any label or per-ceived difference. We need to make an effort to get to know each student as an individual with passions and hatreds, strengths and weaknesses. Too often students with significant learning struggles are used to being treated differently, significantly so, from their peers. They hear euphemisms for themselves and their peers that signal they are different than the general education population — names such as "bus kids" or "IEP students" mark their iden-tity. We need to be sure that these students know we see them.

If you haven't already done so, you will want to build a writing community that celebrates differences and fosters risk-taking. I'm not sure if it was the inimitable Maxine Green or someone else who said, "There's no such thing as a safe classroom. We can't promise it and, quite frankly, learning is not safe. But what we can do is cultivate a risk-taking classroom, where risk-taking is encouraged and expected." As part of that risk-taking, we want students to learn to celebrate successes, yes, but also to celebrate failures as opportunities for learning. Additionally, classrooms where students' differences are frequently discussed and admired are also important. While this is certainly something all of us should do, no matter what our classroom makeup is, it's absolutely vital that we do this if we know we have students with significant writing, or any other type of learning challenges. A few ways to do this include:

- Consider giving students surveys so that they get a sense of what their strengths and challenges are in writing. (See Figure 6–1.)

- Set aside time regularly to share the struggles of professional writers that they know. Then offer time for students to share stories of their own struggles.

- Ensure that students have opportunities to work with a variety of people *and* also build long-term working relationships with a few people as well. Many

Figure 6–1 Student Writing Survey

Name: _____

Please answer each question as honestly as you can. Your answers will help me be a better writing teacher for you. Also, feel free to change or revise any questions as needed.

	Always	Often	Sometimes	Rarely	Never
I enjoy writing.					
My hand hurts when I write.					
My hand gets tired when I write.					
I have an easy time coming up with ideas to write about.					
I have a hard time explaining what I am trying to say in writing.					
Remembering how to spell words is easy for me.					
I forget about punctuation.					
I feel comfortable with grammar in writing.					
I like writing about my life and my feelings.					
I enjoy writing stories.					
I enjoy writing informational (nonfiction) pieces.					
I enjoy writing essays and other pieces where I share my opinions.					
I have a hard time including research in my writing.					
I enjoy describing things and using lots of details in my writing.					
It is hard for me to choose the right words.					
I like sharing my writing with others.					
I like to see my writing hanging on a bulletin board.					
Using a checklist helps me with my writing.					

Anything else you would like me to know about you as a writer?

© 2015 from *The Unstoppable Writing Teacher* by M. Colleen Cruz. Heinemann: Portsmouth, NH.

teachers regularly change seats, table-groupings, and talk partners to allow for maximum experiences. I would also argue that it is important for writing partners, once they have been well matched, to stick together throughout the year. Working with someone on your writing gets better over the long haul, after you've gotten to know someone's strengths and quirks. This also fosters risk-taking as they become more and more familiar with each other.

Of course, the greatest community in the world won't help a student improve his writing if he's not writing. We must ensure that students have the maximum amount of time writing we can give. This tip might seem to be an extremely obvious one. However, one of the things I noticed in my own classroom and I notice quite a bit as I travel through other people's classrooms, is that the students who most need time to write independently have the least amount of time. This is either because they are not in classroom during writing workshop and are receiving services for another subject elsewhere, or else, there are so many grownups to support them that they rarely write a sentence without an audience. If you are able to do nothing else from this chapter to help your writers with the biggest challenges, *please try to hold independent writing time sacred.* Try to make sure that these students have a regular daily (or almost daily) writing time that they can count on. It is very difficult to get stronger at something that one does not practice on a consistent and regular basis.

Additionally, you will want to study the students closely—as if you know nothing about them. Many teachers have told me that one of the most important things they do as educators is to approach their new class each year without any preconceived notions. This is no easy feat. Between cumulative files, reorganization cards, and countless conversations between colleagues, we likely have some ideas about the students who will be sitting in our classroom before they ever step foot inside. Rather than ignore all that information, consider adding to it. Observe the student in a variety of situations. Listen to her talk to her friends over snack. Pay attention to what she does with her feet during writing time. What does her pencil grip look like? Notice where her eyes are and aren't during writing time. Look for patterns across the topics she chooses to write about. (See Figure 6–2.) These bits of information will help add layers of knowledge, which ultimately helps you move this child as a writer.

Once you've done your research you'll want to build theories and try them. This is perhaps the hardest thing for those of us who like to be 100 percent sure of something before we try it. However, this is one of the biggest reasons why teaching is an art form. Sometimes we just have to go with what our brains and hearts are saying a child might need. If we notice that a child holds her head a little too close to the paper, we might suggest that her family get her eyes examined. If we notice that a child tells a great, complicated story, but his writing is never longer than a couple of sentences, we might suggest that he rehearse his

Figure 6–2 Observation Note-Taking

Notes about _____

Social conversation	Whole-class conversation	Small-group conversation	Pen grip	Feet placement
Closeness of face to paper (vision)	Legibility and size of writing	Pressure on pen	Eyes during workshop (on charts, on own work, on classmates' work, wandering, reading, etc.)	Posture
Patterns of getting started in writing	Patterns in topics	Patterns in strategies	Subject areas of strength	Subject areas of struggle
When experiencing success . . .	When experiencing frustration . . .	Areas of expertise	Spelling	Grammar

© 2015 from *The Unstoppable Writing Teacher* by M. Colleen Cruz. Heinemann: Portsmouth, NH.

stories orally before he writes. These are all just theories. Some might be wrong, some might be right. As long as the theory a teacher chooses to test out is based on her knowledge of the student, is not harmful, is as unobtrusive as possible, and supports independence, we can rest assured that a little trial and error is a good thing.

Additionally, if you haven't already done so, you might want to explore Universal Design for Learning (UDL)—a teaching framework designed to support all learners, with a range of strengths and challenges. There is much more to the framework than can be discussed fully in this book, and I highly encourage you to do some professional reading on the topic if you aren't familiar with it (I suggest *Universal Design for Learning in the Classroom* edited by Anne Meyer, Tracey Hall, and David Rose). Suffice it to say, in the UDL framework, rather than simply differentiating tasks for students, teachers aim to teach an accessible strategy or concept that allows multiple pathways of accessibility. This means that you might instead aim for something broader, focusing more on the bigger concepts in your lessons, offering students a wide variety of strategies for accessing those concepts. It takes into account three brain networks: recognition, strategic, and affective. By considering how humans take in and represent information, how they learn and accomplish things, and how they can best be engaged and autonomous, UDL is an excellent framework for those of us who teach a wide range of learners.(Also see Figure 6–3.)

You might find after you've tried all the strategies you could come up with on your own that you need to enlist help. Good for you. There are so many educators with vast experiences working with the kinds of students who need us most. Likely there are many in your building. Lots in your district. Tons in your state. Countless online. I know I frequently asked around for information and suggestions any chance I could. I was particularly fond of asking service providers. Physical therapists taught me more than I thought possible about the mind-body connection. Speech therapists taught me so much about the connections between memory and language processing. My goldmines are occupational therapists. If I meet one out and about socially—look out, I will be asking them questions for the rest of the night. What can I do to help someone focus when something is hard? Are there tools I should bring into my room to help students who have fine motor weakness? How can my room environment support students with sensory issues while still being stimulating to kids who need that? Are there language structures universal enough that I should teach them to everyone? Even when I am hesitant about asking for help or who to ask, I would ask those closest to me, "Do you know who I should talk to about . . . ?" and they inevitably know.

Additionally, don't be afraid to ask for other kinds of help—not just of the information and advice kind. When one of my students was hospitalized for a mental illness and returned to the classroom later, I spoke to my administrator and school guidance counselor to help put together a support plan for the student as well as the rest of my class. It involved the guidance counselor helping me plan what to say to my students to prepare them for their classmate's return, and sitting beside me as I ran the conversation. We also worked together to create a safety plan so that I had a signal I could send via phone to any administrator and to the security desk in case of emergency.

When I felt like the high needs level of my students was wearing me out, I asked for additional supports, extra hands in the classroom, and additional training, to help me make it through the year. There are no blue ribbons for burnt-out teachers. But there are lots of rewards for those who take care of themselves as well as their students and are able to stay in the game as long as they want.

Figure 6–3 Writing Instruction Informed by Three Brain Networks

Brain Network	What It Does	What It Could Look Like to Teach & Learn with Consideration to Brain Networks
Recognition	It handles the content of learning—how we take in information.	• When teaching a writing lesson, make sure to not just teach it orally, but also use images and gestures. • Tailor teaching tools to students' needs. For example, for some students writing strategy charts would be easier to learn from if they were shrunk down and placed on stands on work tables. • Use music, video, amplified voice to add auditory and visual options for learning about language.
Strategic	It handles the ways we learn—the planning and performing of tasks.	• Actively teach a variety of options for the writing process. Students can learn which parts of the process they should tweak and which they shouldn't. They can also learn how to move themselves independently through the process. • Give students choice in planning methods: graphic organizers, outlines, and oral rehearsal, for example. • Offer choices in writing tools: paper with different line width, pen options, room for sketching, or technology. • Seek out options for presenting finished writing pieces such as illustrated, digital, audio recorded, etc.
Affective	It handles the reasons we learn—interest, motivation, the love of a challenge.	• Actively work to engage student interest in writing projects by using compelling examples. • Increase the level of autonomy and purpose by grounding writing in real-world audiences and uses. • Co-create systems of self-monitoring and problem solving so that students have a clear vision for their writing and are not deterred by struggle.

✳ Ongoing Work: Growth Doesn't Always Show Up When We Want It To

Unfortunately, this is entirely possible. You worked your way through the list of suggestions. You kept your game face on. You never gave up. You were unstoppable. But, when you did stop and you read that student's most recent work, you noticed no improvement. Or, perhaps even worse, a backslide. If that's the case there are a few suggestions I might make to you:

1. Take a break. Sometimes we have been working too hard and focused too much on one student or one issue. It might help everyone involved to step back, put the work on hold, and get a fresh pair of eyes to come back and try again later.

2. Revisit the list of things you can do again. Sometimes there might be one you haven't yet tried. Perhaps there was an expert you haven't spoken to. A family member who holds a key.

3. Keep things in perspective. With the student, focus on the areas where he has grown in writing, even if they're microscopic, and name them. Look at word count, use of endpoints, vocabulary, purpose, or voice. Remember that, despite all the voices going on around us, not every child is ready for what other people want him to be ready for *right now.* What you and the student should be after is that the student is learning and growing. We are not only looking for strong writing. We are also hoping to help this student learn to use writing as a tool she can use for life to help her make meaning, develop her identity, and communicate with others.

I remember before I made my final decision to work with students who receive special education services, I called my mentor, a staff developer with many years of experience. "I don't know if I can do this," I remember saying into the phone. She laughed and said, "You can teach kids, right?" "Yes," I said. "And you like kids, right?" "Of course," I said. "Well, they're just kids. They're only special ed kids in school. At home, on the street, on the playground, they're just kids. You know how to teach kids."

This felt very profound to me. They're just kids. And I know how to teach kids. There are many things that this student can and does do well. Perhaps this writing piece, perhaps writing itself, is just not what he's ready for right now. And that's okay. That doesn't mean we need to give up. It just means we need to give it another try.

7

"I never have enough time."

Recently I sat with a group of teachers and their calendars trying to decipher when they could schedule the launch of their latest writing unit. All of them needed to teach reading, writing, and math daily. They also endeavored to teach another subject like social studies or science. This didn't take into account other subjects like spelling, art, or conflict resolution. They also had no control over other activities they needed to fit into their days such as band practice, pullout service programs, special assemblies, announcements, chess lessons, or ballroom dancing. All of these were great things that the teachers loved for their students, but when combining those special events, their academic demands, and the time stealers of packing up, bathroom visits, behavioral distractions, and fire drills, there was just no imagining when they could fit in a launch without something radical changing.

I have never met a teacher who has uttered, "I just have so much time, I don't know how I will possibly fill it!"

It's such a universal reality that Lucy Calkins has called finding time to teach a professional hazard. Every profession has its hazards. For firefighters, the hazard is the fire and the dangers inherent in that. For doctors the occupational hazard is that people die. No matter how great a doctor you are, eventually you will have patients who die. For teachers, our issue is time. There is a world to teach out there and we will never have enough time to teach everything we would like to teach.

✳ What Stops Us: We Don't Have Time to Reflect

Throughout this book, I have endeavored to address the issues I most commonly see getting in the way of strong and committed teachers. However, I fully acknowledge that almost every reader of this book will decide to skip at least one chapter, because it just doesn't apply to them. The lack of time, however, is the only problem that every teacher, in every state and every country I have worked in, has felt stopped by.

When schools or individuals move toward teaching using the workshop models, one of the first things they want is professional time outside of the classroom in order to plan, read student work, find mentor texts, and meet with colleagues. However, much of the professional time during the school day is often already accounted for. Teachers can find themselves inspired and ready to dig in, but also needing to find the time to do so.

One of the biggest issues with lack of time is that teachers also need time to actually teach. However, when whittling a schedule, often the first R to drop from the three Rs is the one that belongs to writing (which, of course, starts with a W . . .). There are many reasons for this; chief among them is that for many schools, math and reading test scores count for more than writing, so things that are not tested get cut first.

It is also often true that there are many demands on our time that we have little or no control over. It's not as if these things have higher value than writing, as much as they are things that are not things we can turn down: a special assembly for bullying, a visitor from the historical society, music lessons, a state-mandated six-week healthy eating program. Entire books can be written about the frustrations of the intercom with interruptions and announcements. One frustrated group of teachers figured out that when they added up the daily five-minute announcements they lost on average an hour and forty minutes a month. That would be more than enough time for two writing workshop sessions.

There's also the added pressure of when there aren't enough minutes in a period, compounded by how many students you have. One of the questions I have been asked most when working on site with teachers and over social media, is how to balance meeting regularly with students one-on-one when there's thirty-some-odd kids and only thirty minutes to write each period. Even if management and interruptions were not an issue, simply getting to each student and having a meaningful conference with them can feel quite daunting.

Probably, most importantly, there needs to be lots of time for students to write. Without regular amounts of time, at least four times a week, for thirty to forty-five minutes, they will not be able to develop their strengths as writers. Instinctively, we know this is true. Yet, because of time being such a precious commodity, one of the first things we give up is student work time. Sometimes this happens because we have fewer teaching minutes in a day than we would hope. Sometimes this happens because our minilesson turns into a giant lesson. Sometimes service providers take students out for their services during their writing time. So crucial is student writing time, that when I visit a building where the teachers say writing workshop isn't working, one of the first things I'll ask to see is the daily schedule and how many minutes a day students get to write. We would never expect a professional athlete to become better without time for practice with a coach. We would never expect a violinist to become a virtuoso without practice and instruction. Yet for many of us, the most precious commodity in our classrooms is time. We never have enough.

✳ See Opportunity: Set Clear Priorities and Boundaries

Time is a slippery thing in the rest of life, so it should not be surprising that it is just as tricky when it comes to the classroom. However, having not enough of anything is one of the most compelling reasons for a person to prioritize. As a teacher, there are so many things that need to happen *right now*. And everything is very important. As I mentioned elsewhere in this book, one of my most profound epiphanies was that it was not possible for me to do everything I was supposed to do. The thing is, for a long time I still tried to do it all. Eventually I realized something was going to have to give. The only way to decide what needs to be pruned is to decipher what is in fact most important — to you, to your students, to your administration. Not having enough time forces your hand to decide on your priorities. If you don't, time will decide for you, and remove the decision from your hands, often leaving out some of the most important stuff.

When you decide to tackle the issue of time, you also attack the issue of values and importance. By reflecting on what really matters in your instruction, what you value most, you will find it much easier to know what deserves more time and what deserves less.

But, perhaps even better than all that reflecting and trimming, is the act of communicating those new priorities and boundaries to the people who matter the most: your students, families, and colleagues. Acknowledging that we have some power in our schedules to decide what is best for our students and then going about making those clear to others will have longer repercussions than simply more time.

✳ Experiment: Plan and Fire-Test Your Teaching

Now that we've acknowledged just how big of a monster time is, and how even thinking about it will likely be transformative, it's also important to say that there are ways to make or find more time for the things that matter most to us.

Perhaps the first thing to do is to create a schedule that holds priority subjects sacred and then stick to it. Mary Ehrenworth has said that our teaching schedule is a moral document. It lets our children know and reminds us of what is most important. When we make time for some things and not time for others we are telling ourselves and everyone else what matters most to us. If you haven't yet done this, create a place on your classroom wall to post your daily agenda. Aim for writing workshop at least four times a week, in blocks of forty to sixty minutes.

In a perfect world, the time of day for writing would stay mostly the same so that when the clock showed that hour the class would become used to naturally moving to that subject. (See Figure 7–1.)

Once you have a schedule that reflects your beliefs, your next step is to go hunting for hidden time. There are edges and nooks and crannies in almost every school day—most of them are ones we can't see right away. One of the best ways I learned to find those precious minutes was taught to me by my principal, Liz Phillips. I made the mistake of complaining to her that I was feeling overwhelmed and couldn't possibly accomplish everything I needed to accomplish in the hours I had in the school day. Her advice was for me to carry a stop-watch (or a cell-phone app) and time how much time was spent on everything in a day. Despite my huffing and puffing, I did as she suggested and to my horror I discovered when I did that was that I was losing almost an hour a day to transitions. Fifteen minutes to unpack in the morning. Ten minutes getting reading for lunch. Ten minutes after lunch. Fifteen minutes packing to go home. With lots of other minutes lost in between. I learned to teach my students how to transition while a two-minute song played, thus saving almost forty

Figure 7–1 Sample Schedule

	Monday	Tuesday	Wednesday	Thursday	Friday
8:20–9:10	Read-Aloud/Word Study	*Spanish*	Reading	Reading	Reading
9:10–10:00	*Gym*	Reading	Math	Math	Math
10:00–10:50	Reading	Math	*Gym*	Writing	Writing
10:50–11:40	Math	Writing	Writing	Read-Aloud/Word Study	*Dance*
11:40–12:30	Lunch	Lunch	Lunch	Lunch	Lunch
12:30–1:20	**Writing**	Read-Aloud/Word Study	Read-Aloud/Word Study	*Library*	Read-Aloud
1:20–2:30	Social Studies	Science	Social Studies	Science	Choice/Projects

* Italics denote prep periods. All other subjects taught by classroom teacher.

minutes of time each day. My guess is that you have your own time Achilles heel. Maybe you spend too much time getting ready for each lesson. Maybe students aren't doing enough to run the classroom and you are doing too much. It could be a whole host of things. The best way to find out is to time yourself for a week, then study the information you find in order to address it. Then be willing to make changes to recoup those lost minutes. A few places you might look to salvage some wasted time:

- **Materials distribution and collection.** You might consider having students do this as they leave or enter the room. Or having students pass out materials while others get started. Or have student mailboxes where materials needed for each day can be distributed by helpers at the start of the day and gathered as needed. Or simply make all materials student accessible, so they can grab them as they need.

- **Waiting time.** Waiting for announcements. Waiting for a special visitor. Waiting for the bathroom. See which of these things can be done more time efficiently and independently.

- **Copying homework.** Unless students need to copy homework for a very particular purpose (like a week of cursive writing practice, or practicing abbreviations and note-taking), most homework can be disseminated in a variety of other ways: jotted as students go through the day, saved on a school website or shared drive like Google Drive, preprinted and distributed, or emailed.

You might also consider fire-testing your teaching. There's an old notion that in order to find out what's really valuable it helps to play the mental game of "what if my house was on fire and I could only grab a few things." The truth is, that game can be played with any concept that needs a little prioritizing. What we teach or do in our classroom is a great example of this. Is it really important to make those Abraham Lincoln hats out of felt for Presidents' Day? Maybe, if that's crucial to your curriculum or is one of your biggest passions. But, I would argue, most of us have several things we teach or do that we continue to do not because they are our life's passion or instrumental to our students' learning, but rather because we've always done them. I have worked with fifth-grade teachers who realized, upon closer examination, that the month-long unit on apple picking, complete with a trip to the orchard and making "Apple People," which had been taught in the building for decades, was better placed in another, younger grade. When we fire-test our teaching, saving only what's essential or enormously valuable, we can often find ourselves with anywhere from several minutes a day (morning recitals of the 4–305 class pledge) to weeks (apple unit) of extra teaching time.

After making all these revisions and clarifications, you will likely want to communicate with people who affect your schedule. There are millions of insidious ways time gets sucked out of our schedules not by our own hands. Morning announcements, assemblies, pullout programs, and mandatory snacks are just a few of the things teachers have named when talking about their frustrations. When I was in the classroom, I was especially frustrated when students who received services were pulled out for things that could just have easily been done inside the classroom. I was complaining to a colleague about this one day when she asked, "Why don't you just ask service providers to push-in when they can?" It seemed so simple, yet there was the perfect solution. I spoke to the service providers who worked with my kids and almost all of them started to push-in at least part time — a huge time saver as well as a boon for integrated services and communication. That simple act can be repeated in almost any situation. Morning announcements taking too long? Perhaps ask if the announcements can be emailed to teachers each morning to share during morning meeting in the classroom and the loud speaker is saved for only emergencies. Assemblies every month are adding up to two weeks of lost teaching time over the school year? One group of third-grade teachers in Brooklyn asked to have these assemblies rescheduled to times when teachers were in professional development or during lunch hours in the cold weather months. No matter what is stealing time from you, it can't hurt to make a suggestion so that less class time is taken.

✳ Ongoing Work: When Time Starts Slipping Again, We Must Catch It

Over the years I have found that time management is a lot like keeping my closets organized. No matter how thoroughly I cleaned the closet in August, by November it is a hot mess. I feel like time is very much the same way. Just as clothing starts to pile up and gather dust, items keep getting added to our schedules as the months pass. We need to make a point of checking in and seeing where we might need to trim again. Have the announcements started back? Have we slipped in our planning and are letting our prep time bleed into our teaching time? No matter what it is, if you went from feeling as if your time was manageable (not perfect—we are not likely to ever be satisfied with the amount of time we have) to suddenly feeling as if you are running on a treadmill again, you will want to see if maybe things need to be reprioritized and new cuts and additions made.

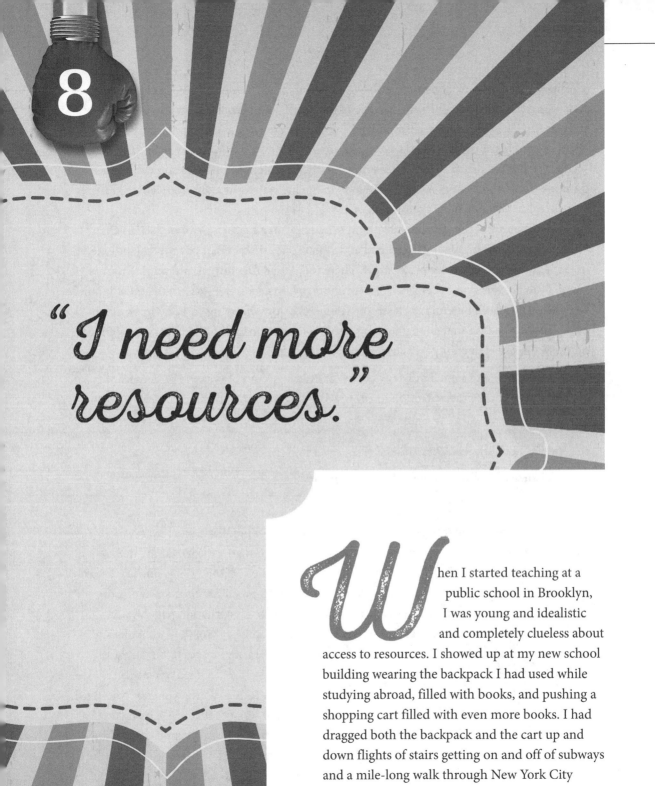

8

"I need more resources."

When I started teaching at a public school in Brooklyn, I was young and idealistic and completely clueless about access to resources. I showed up at my new school building wearing the backpack I had used while studying abroad, filled with books, and pushing a shopping cart filled with even more books. I had dragged both the backpack and the cart up and down flights of stairs getting on and off of subways and a mile-long walk through New York City streets.

The Assistant Principal met me at the school door with a smile. "Let me take you to your classroom!" he said, running off down the hall before I could catch my breath. I lugged my stuff up three more flights of stairs only to find my classroom was empty. Actually empty. Not a stick of furniture was inside. No desks, no bookshelves, nothing. My new AP didn't seem to notice my distress. "We'll head down to the basement to find you some desks. I think we ordered new ones. And we can look in the hallway for bookshelves. There are always some that someone is getting rid of."

I spent the rest of the afternoon, with my AP's help, lugging thirty-two desks and chairs up from the basement. By the time I had added four bookshelves that I'd found abandoned in the hallways, I was feeling pretty great. There was actual furniture in my very own class-room. I didn't even stop to consider that furniture, while necessary, was not the most impor-tant material I could have in my classroom. I unpacked my shopping cart and book-filled backpack only to find that all that lugging resulted in only one shelf filled. My voice echoed off the walls it was so empty. My classroom still needed:

- Books. There were hardly any books for the classroom library. No textbooks. No teacher's guides. Nothing with words written on it.

- Paper.

- Chalk or whiteboard markers.

- Pencils or pens — or any school supplies at all.

- Curriculum.

My AP assured me that the school would be distributing supplies in the next few days, along with the scope and sequence of what I would be teaching that year. But the next day, when he showed up again at my door with my box of supplies, all that was inside was a box of chalk, an eraser, some permanent markers, about fifty #2 pencils, a class-sized box of crayons, five glue sticks, a few packs of lined paper, a pack of construction paper, some paint, and three pads of chart paper. He later returned with a box of math workbooks and some sheets of paper, one for each subject. They contained a list of topics to be taught in each subject area. Needless to say, I was missing some things I would need to teach.

This was at a time in New York City where teachers new to the system were not paid until Thanksgiving break. I was fresh out of graduate school and was not flush with cash. Yet, I needed books and notebooks and more paper, not to mention other art supplies and things that would just make the room feel right. In the next few months the school was able to fill a few gaps (including showing me where the book room was to help fill my library shelves), but by Thanksgiving I had maxed out almost all of my credit cards.

Now, to be fair, what my school at that time did not have in terms of physical resources, it more than made up for in collegial ones. I was surrounded by some of the smartest, most generous educators in the world. But there were plenty of ways that year where I felt the lack of physical resources deeply. And in the almost two decades since, in many different situations and positions, I have either felt or witnessed the daily struggle to teach writing well when a teacher lacks the resources he needs.

✳ What Stops Us: It's Hard to Imagine Doing Without

Resources cover a lot of different things. For the purposes of this book I see resources mainly as materials and human support. Simply thinking of Maslow's hierarchy of needs, we know that unless we have our most basic needs met (air, food, shelter), we cannot possibly begin to consider other steps such as friendship, let alone self-actualization. For a teacher and her students, not having resources can make it very difficult, if not impossible, to get to the highest levels of academic achievement. How can we possibly teach writing without *paper*?

Without materials like paper, pens, or for higher-tech schools, laptops, printers, and tablets, students cannot produce the work we know they are capable of producing. We need to have enough so that students can write as many drafts as they need to, recycle as many pages as they publish. Ideally we'd like enough resources to give students choices in the types of writing implements and paper they use so their medium can match their message and vision as much as possible.

Books are one of the first resources teachers almost universally want, whether or not they are teaching writing workshop. We know reading is the most powerful activity our students can do. Complicate that with the fact that our students regularly look to books and other texts as inspirations for writing projects, ideas for craft moves, confirmation of grammar rules. Professionally published texts become our students' mentors. Without mentor texts in the classroom it is difficult for students to envision possibilities for their own projects. A lack of mentor texts can also keep teachers from imagining alternative teaching points for students who need them.

I knew as a teacher that resources could make or break my teaching. I knew that telling students we couldn't try or do something because we just didn't have it was one of the hardest things I could do. So, I made myself broke trying to cover all those needs myself my first year. Just recently though, through the eyes of a parent, I realized why I felt so passionately about providing so many resources. I watched as my older son finished drawing a picture. He got up from the table and headed to a shelf to get more paper. All in a rush I remembered myself as a child, knowing that there was a limit to how much paper I could use at any given point. My parents were great about taking me to the library and anything else that was free, but materials like paper were finite resources. So much so that I needed to stem my dreams for projects in order to make them stretch as long as possible. I am fortunately not in the same financial straits as my parents were and paper is by no means a limited resource for my own children. But, in that moment of gratitude of what I could offer my own children, I realized why I so passionately wanted to offer as much to my students. I never wanted resources to get in the way of their capabilities.

On the other side, I feel that it is also important to say, that as with most things, but is especially obvious with resources, there is always somebody in the world who has it worse. I have met a teacher who taught a class of 100 refugees in tents using the tent flaps as teaching space and the students wrote with sticks in the dry earth. I have worked with teachers who know that when school is closed on the weekends and over vacations, their students do not eat, so they make sure students go home with snack bags of granola bars, fruit, and peanut butter. Sometimes just being aware of the fact that it could actually be worse can make dealing with what we do have just a little bit easier.

✳ See Opportunity: Widen Our Community by Asking and Sharing

It would be very easy to just throw up your hands and say, "We'll just make do with what we have." And that certainly is an option if the resources, while lean, might be just enough to do what you want and need to do for the teaching of writing. Or, if you just have other bigger issues to contend with and plan to get to the issue of resources when you are through putting out bigger fires. After all, some resources are more important than others. But, for those of you who are tempted to give up your dreams of writing workshop because of resources, there are a few very good reasons to fight the fight.

Gathering resources is one of the quickest things to accomplish on your unstoppable teacher checklist. Unlike many of the other topics in this book, you will likely see payoff right away. Which will not only give you more resources, but might be the energy boost you need to tackle other problems. A lot of resources are tangible. There is something intensely satisfying about putting one's hands on a stack of freshly gathered books for the classroom library, or the smell of newly unwrapped school supplies. There's a simple joy in that which makes all of this a lot more fun.

Your kids need things in order to become the writers you know they can be. Sometimes these things are purely practical — like lined white paper or a printer that actually prints. Other times they are things that are inspirational and aspirational: thick creamy parchment paper for historical fiction; sparkly gel pens for fantasy stories; calligraphy pens for the perfect covers; Bare Books for that "real hard-cover book" feeling. No matter what the stuff is, it can actually make a huge difference in not only the work a student can produce but also allow him to more closely match the vision of how the work should be received by his audience.

Can an argument be made that "stuff" is not as important as the learning or work a student or writer does? Absolutely. But, it is also true that materials can be tied to our identity as students, teachers, writers, and artists. Just as German school children are traditionally given a *schulüte* (a cone filled with school supplies and treats) and Japanese children are given *randoseru* (a sturdy leather backpack) as they start first grade to signify they have officially become students, we too want our writers to have those signalers of identity. We would be lying to ourselves if we said we don't identify certain objects or materials with certain phases or life, certain identities. (Go ahead—think of three professions and try to imagine them without some sort of material objects involved: plumber, with a plunger; doctor, with a stethoscope; artist, with a paintbrush.) The writing pens they hold, the access to the perfect mentor texts, the choice of just the right paper, signal that these are not the supplies for just anyone. These are the supplies of *writers*.

Sharing our stories of overcoming the resource obstacle is often the one story that other people (parents, students, fellow teachers) are dying to hear. Everyone is lacking in one resource or another, so by cracking the resource code and sharing it with others you are also enabling them to do the same in their own lives.

✳ Experiment: Harvest Materials from Everywhere

I know that many people believe that less is more, that more things (whether laser printers or more professional literature) do not a great classroom make. I agree with that. And, I also know that in classrooms that are really rocking and rolling with writing workshop, teachers often have enough of the resources that they need in order to do the work they want to do.

The fantastic news about getting resources for your classroom is that there is actually quite a bit you can do, much of it by yourself, and right away.

One of my favorite things to do right away because it takes very little effort and no money is to make a wish list. A surprising number of people, even in very underserved communities, have access to the materials you need. When you send out your supply list for the year, consider tacking on a wish list at the end. You never know whose uncle might work for 3-M, after all! It's also true that when a family is shopping for supplies for an individual child, they might see a great sale on exactly the items you need (ten-cent notebooks! one-cent pens!) and can pick them up for pennies. It is important that you consider whether or not making a class wish list that families see is a good idea or not. In some areas it might put pressure on families who are not able to give. In other communities, especially if your wish list is very diverse (paper clips, folders, scrap paper, highlighters, empty plastic bottles to turn into supply jars, etc.), families will welcome the opportunity to contribute.

Additionally, many online companies and brick-and-mortar stores offer options for teachers to create and post their wish lists. Local book and stationery stores are a great place to post your list — tell your friends and students about the list — but also be prepared for the possibility that generous strangers might throw a few things your way. Amazon wish lists allow teachers to include everything from a ream of paper to beanbag chairs on the same list.

Another option is to consider trading resources with others. This was something I did fairly regularly when I was still in the classroom. My colleagues and I would convene in someone's classroom after school, toting our "extras." These were items that for whatever reason we had too many of. I always had too many paintbrushes and construction paper and not enough pens. My colleague across the hall had too many pens and premade picture paper, but was in dire need of rulers. By swapping around with each other, we off-loaded our surplus and gained some of the crucial supplies we needed most.

You might also consider attending more professional development workshops, conferences, and literacy fairs. Often these events, organized and provided for teachers, are chock-full of materials giveaways and resource lists. Every time I attend a national conference I bring a full-size empty suitcase that I stuff with the books, pencils, notebooks, posters, and sample materials I have collected.

Another popular option is to hit up teacher giveaway organizations. We live in a great age of information access. One of the best things about this is that it is easier than ever to find donors who are looking to give a teacher the materials he most needs. Some of the most famous ones, like Donors Choose and First Book, are dedicated to helping out teachers who work in underserved communities. Others give away materials to anyone who applies. In addition to doing a quick Internet search for these organizations, a few of my favorites are listed below:

- **First Book** provides books for children in need. There is an easy, quick grant application to fill out. www.firstbook.org

- **Adopt A Classroom** gives donors an opportunity to donate money to a teacher they know, a school they have a connection with, or a project they love. Teachers are then able to shop online with the funds. One hundred percent of the money raised goes to the classrooms. www.adoptaclassroom.org

- **Donors Choose** is very similar to Adopt A Classroom. Except instead of the teacher shopping for the materials, she makes her order before the funds are received. If the project is funded, Donors Choose sends the materials to the teacher's school. www.donorschoose.com

✳ Ongoing Work: I Feel Like It's a Bottomless Pit

Here's the thing about resources: once you have cracked the code on some (time, the perfect donor organization, the best place to post your wish list), you'll find you have an endless access to those resources and you will no longer have to think about them. Other resources, especially consumables like paper and pens, will be hard to come by for free and will be a constant source of scrambling and thoughts. If that is the case for you, and this is the thing that is making you question your ability to stay in the classroom, then I recommend having a conversation with whoever in your building holds the purse strings. Every school has a budget. Speak with this person about either expanding existing budget lines or else adding a new one to incorporate the costs of those things you are unable to procure in other ways. Depending on who you need to speak with, it might help make your case more convincing if you also share all of the things you have done to make sure other resources are provided for. Often this upfront and teamwork attitude is appreciated.

If, for whatever reason, the budget cannot be revised in order to include the needs you and your colleagues have, you might suggest some fundraising opportunities. Bake sales are obvious choices, of course. But so are things related to writing and the work your students do. Perhaps you can sell students' published work? Maybe you can have students design and advertise something to sell. No matter what you decide, do know that with a little creativity and a few volunteers you might very well be able to get the cash you need to realize your hopes.

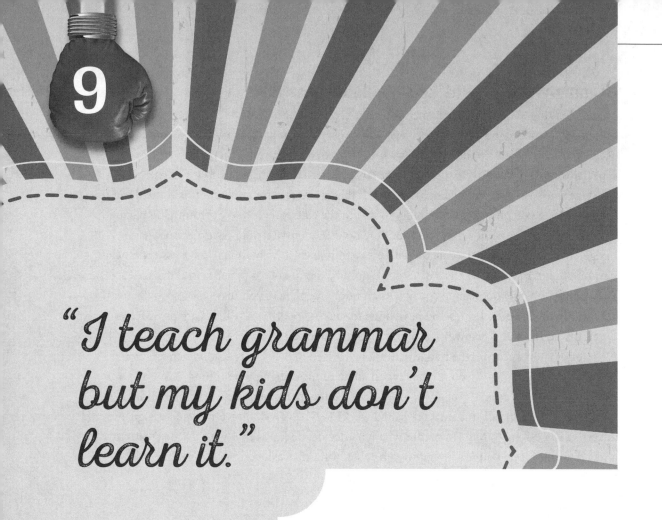

9

"I teach grammar but my kids don't learn it."

ull disclosure: I am a full-fledged grammar nerd. I love grammar. I love punctuation. I love knowing the stories behind the history of how our language evolved. I can't help but notice interesting grammar evolutions (like the way *-ly* seems to be slowly dropping off of many adverbs). I have favorite grammar books that I read for fun.

Seriously.

When I was writing a book for Heinemann a few years ago, my editor at the time, knowing my grammar passion, emailed me excitedly that for my latest book I was going to get the best copyeditor they had. I was thrilled. She then forwarded me an email that copyeditor sent her along with my edits. "This is the cleanest [least error-riddled] copy I've seen in a while." I glowed with pride. Until I opened the document. Every page was covered in corrections. If this was clean, I would hate to see dirty.

The point of me telling you this is that I know the hunger that is teaching grammar. I also know the exhausted feeling of seeing student writing with little command of conventions *that I just taught*: third-graders writing without capital letters at the start of sentences; fourth-graders writing without periods; fifth-graders writing endless run-on sentences . . .

I also know that if there is one criticism of writing workshop that drives me the most batty, it's that some people believe workshop teachers don't explicitly teach grammar. Meanwhile, I have yet to meet a teacher who has not done some serious thinking and hard work in the name of teaching students conventional writing.

✳ What Stops Us: Everyone Thinks They Know Everything About Something Very Few People Actually Know

It seems that no one has it easy in the world of grammar instruction. For those of us who shudder every time we read "she ran quick," there are just as many of us who shudder when we hear the term "adverbs of manner." (What does *that* mean?!) There are many, many reasons why teaching grammar is troublesome. Not the least of which is our own personal relationship with grammar. Some of us found grammar a logical, predictable concept in the constantly changing sea of the writing world. Others of us had humiliating experiences that are directly connected with grammar goof-ups. Still others have no scars, but we know that our depth of knowledge isn't the deepest, and so we break out in hives when even considering the semicolon.

Grammar is fraught with expectations. Often the adults outside of the classroom (parents, grandfathers, older sisters, administrators) will call out grammar, and its first cousin spelling, as the things they can see that need to be worked on in a child's writing. Other areas of instruction like craft, elaboration, structure, and genre knowledge just don't jump out at people as much as a missing capital letter or an overlong sentence. Because of that jumping-out quality, there's an assumption that, when it comes to grammar, anything that's not done in a standard way should be "fixed" right away. "How come they don't know how to do this *now*?" they'll wonder.

For many of those folks, there's very little consideration or awareness of a student's developmental level, or that there is even a developmental range inside of grammar. Third-graders have no reason to be concerning themselves with attending to run-on sentences, when they are still working on pronoun antecedents, for example. These very high expectations—and in my opinion, unrealistic — will be incredibly challenging to meet. Additionally, they can cast a dark pall over every piece hung on a bulletin board with grammatical errors.

Then there's the fact, like in every other subject we teach, students' grammar and conventions knowledge tends to run from one end of the spectrum to the other. For every fourth-grader struggling with simple sentences and forgetting to indent paragraphs, there's another one who writes with grammatical-abandon, stringing together phrases, clauses, and fancy punctuation to write paragraph-long sentences that are almost impossible to untangle. Trying to find a balance between teaching the basics to students who need them and teaching the finer nuances of grammar to those who are begging for them can get complicated quickly.

Possibly one of, if not the most frustrating thing about grammar in the writing workshop, is that it seems that even if a teacher manages to clear all the hurdles mentioned above, there is still the problem of retention and application. I have watched teachers almost in tears as they read through final published pieces. "But, I taught paragraphs! No one has paragraphs," they'll exclaim. "How many times did we talk about *was* and *were*?" they'll cry. "No, it can't be . . . lower case *i* . . ." they'll whimper. Teachers are used to teaching and telling things over and over again. It's part of what we do. But it almost seems as if whenever some of us teach grammar, the class is hit with a massive case of amnesia right before they finish their pieces. Nothing seems to be as forgettable as grammar.

Add to the mix that it is not exactly as if students are clamoring to study grammar. Many a child (and grownup) has her eyes glaze over as soon as someone mentions prepositional phrases or transitional conjunctions. It begins to make even the most devoted teacher of writing wonder if it's worth taking time out of an already jam-packed schedule to teach a lesson on misplaced modifiers.

Teaching grammar can quickly turn into a hot mess.

✳ See Opportunity: Unlock the Connection Between Grammar and Meaning

There are plenty of people in the world who feel like grammar is too hard to teach; it becomes an obstacle to so many students trying to get their ideas out, not to mention it can easily be corrected by word-processing programs — so why bother dealing with it? I certainly was in that camp at one point in my teaching career. However, I have come to realize that students benefit greatly when they learn how to use grammar and conventions as part of their writing workshop curriculum.

As much as we wish it were otherwise, people are judged on the way they present themselves. If I show up to a job interview wearing flip-flops, there's a good chance I'm doing damage to my chances to get that job. In some ways, grammar and conventions are the writing equivalent of flip-flops at a job interview. People read expecting a certain knowledge from a writer, and when writers (adult or kid) make errors that feel as if they should know better, the message the writer is trying to get across can get lost. In fact, research has shown that good grammar is a fairly good indicator of professional success in adults. While I wish this wasn't the case, it is. With that in mind, I try to make sure that students learn what they need to know so that as little as possible gets in the way of the ideas they are trying to convey.

Another reason why teaching grammar is worth the trouble is that it is fairly easy to help students retain the grammar we've taught, despite the grammar memory hole many of us have imagined existing in many a student skull. In fact, research has shown that students between the ages of five and sixteen learn grammar and conventions well and have a higher level of transference when it is taught not with textbooks and worksheets, but rather through composition, or writing workshop (York University, 2004). This is just one study. There are many more that show similar things. When we teach a thoughtful, well-planned curriculum using a variety of methods and engaging purposes for the use of conventional English, students and families can see growth quickly and exponentially.

Additionally, unlike a few other things recommended in this book, grammar instruction is fairly easy to tuck into a well-rounded writing workshop. It doesn't need to take up additional time. There's no need to have a special separate time for grammar worksheets, Daily Oral Language, or the like. The beauty of grammar and conventions in the writing workshop is that they go together like a hand in glove.

✻ Experiment: Demonstrate, Share Mentor Texts

"They just don't seem to get quotation marks around dialogue," said Natalie, one of the teachers on the third-grade team at P.S. 295 in Brooklyn. It was October. They had taught minilessons on using quotation marks and pointed them out in mentor texts, but still, while the students were occasionally remembering there should be a comma somewhere near the end quotation mark, they couldn't seem to remember where it went.

"Yeah," Colleen, another third-grade teacher added. "It's like they're doing what I remember doing when I was a kid. They're putting the comma directly under the quotation mark, hoping I won't notice that they don't really know where it goes." We couldn't help but smile at the rather intelligent strategy to deal with that tricky comma placement.

"Can we try an inquiry?" Demaris asked. In a flurry of paper we threw our original lab-site plans out the window and decided to design an inquiry around commas and quotation marks. We created a chart and gathered sticky notes for kids to collect and study their findings. We gathered the students on the rug and told them, "Today we are going to go on an investigation! We are going to look in our independent reading books and find every example we can of an author using quotation marks and commas. Then we're going to collect those together with our table groups and see what kind of patterns we can find." The students tittered in excitement. We upped the excitement even more by passing out giant sticky notes for each table to record their findings. (See Figure 9–1.)

What was most fascinating about doing this inquiry work was not that the students were enthralled and engaged as they pored over their books looking for quotation marks. It was what they were seeing, not seeing, and saying about what they saw. Students who seemed to have the most trouble with finding instances of quotation marks and commas, even when there were several on the page of the book they were studying, were also the least likely to have evidence of them in their writing. Students who were running out of room on their sticky notes and asking for more, were the ones who seemed to have the most conventional use of quotation marks and commas.

When students were finished collecting and discussing patterns they saw, we all returned to the rug to share and reflect. Looking across their collection, students immediately saw a pattern. "A lot of the times, when there's a comma with a quotation mark, the comma is *inside* the quotation mark," one student said. Another piped in, "And, usually after the comma and the quotation mark the book was like 'she said.' It was always 'said' or 'says.' Never 'yelled' or 'asked.'" By the end of our time together, one of the conclusions the students had drawn was that if a writer was writing dialogue and wanted to use a 'said,' the writer would probably want to use a comma right before they closed with a quotation mark.

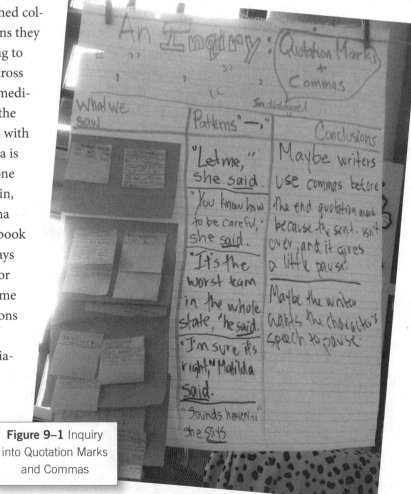

Figure 9–1 Inquiry into Quotation Marks and Commas

The teachers ended our session feeling pretty positive about many of the students' discoveries. They also felt like this was another layer added to students' knowledge about grammar—the first of many they would add during the year.

This inquiry lesson was clearly not the first step toward teaching grammar effectively in a writing workshop classroom. Perhaps the first and most important thing for you to consider is whether or not your school (or district) has a grammar scope and sequence. This is incredibly important. Without this, it is very hard to pass go and collect $200. I have come to believe that it's one of the primary reasons grammar and conventions don't stick for kids. In many buildings every teacher is trying to teach everything. And clearly that's not possible.

In order to teach almost anything well, but particularly grammar, the best way to do it is to have a discrete number of concepts or skills to focus on, to revisit with various teaching methods, and to hold students accountable for learning. What often happens instead is that the second-grade teachers, for example, know that their students need a lot, so they are teaching paragraphing and noun-verb agreement and pronoun antecedents, as well as sentence construction and conjunctions and . . . By the time the year is over, they have *covered* a lot, but students haven't had an opportunity for meaningful repeated practice or the coaching they might need to master those concepts because there's simply too much. Some of it is below their developmental level, some of it above, some of it just right. When the students have gotten to third grade, they haven't really mastered much, but they have been exposed to a lot. So the third-grade teachers, seeing that their students need a lot, begin to cover a lot. And the cycle continues. I tend to agree with what Mary Ehrenworth and Vicki Vinton espouse in their book *The Power of Grammar.* They suggest that schools make sure that every teacher is clear on what they are responsible for teaching each grade. Some things might be simply introduced. Some might be practiced. Other years can expect to work toward mastery. Some years will do all of the above or a combination.

Many schools I have worked with say that either they don't have a scope and sequence for grammar, or the one they have comes from their textbook or some other outside source and doesn't accurately reflect their student community or needs. I suggest that the first step you and your colleagues might want to take is to create a grammar committee or study group. The group might begin by simply surveying their grade-level colleagues about what they plan to teach, know they teach, and wish they didn't have to teach. (See Figure 9–2.)

Using that information, plus the standards your school follows (Common Core Standards, state standards, International Baccalaureate, etc.), you and your team can align and choose the scope and sequence for your building. You might decide that trying to do all of the standards the first year out is a bit much. If that's the case, many schools I've worked with have had four to six starred topics on each grade that the teachers will aim for students to master and other ones that might be simply introduced or practiced. Ehrenworth

Figure 9–2 Teacher Grammar Survey

Dear Colleague,

We are trying to get a sense of everyone's instruction in grammar so that we can create a more cohesive grammar program in our school. Can you please take a few minutes to answer the following questions? Many thanks!

1. What grade do you teach?

2. What grammar and conventions skills do you teach or plan to teach this year?

3. What grammar and conventions skills do you wish students knew before they came to your grade?

4. What grammar or conventions topics do you think are most important to teach in your grade?

5. What grammar and conventions do you feel confident a majority of your students will leave your classroom having mastered?

6. What instructional materials, methods, or approaches do you use to teach grammar? Please describe.

and Vinton offer a very practical method for crafting a sequence that should work for your building.

Once you have a road map, it's time for each individual grade and/or teacher to make the GPS to guide her students to what they need to know. This means deciding on which grammar and conventions skills would be taught when and how in the curriculum. Ehrenworth and Vinton recommend teaching in a spiral fashion, moving backward through the steps of the writing process, as shown in Figure 9–3.

Figure 9–3 Spiral Model for Grammar Instruction

	Unit 1	Unit 2	Unit 3	Unit 4	Unit 5	Unit 6	Unit 7
Freewriting		**Lesson 1** (Ending Punctuation): Writers make choices about ending punctuation while writing. **Lesson 2** (Paragraphing): Fluent writers break their writing into chunks as they write	**Lesson 3** (Subject and Predicate): Fluent writers mostly compose in complete sentences when writing prose. **Lesson 4** (Fragments): Writers, if they use fragments, do so knowingly, purposefully, and sparingly.	**Lesson 3** (Subject and Predicate): Fluent writers mostly compose in complete sentences when writing prose. **Lesson 4** (Fragments): Writers, if they use fragments, do so knowingly, purposefully, and sparingly.	**Lesson 5** (Subject-Verb Agreement): Writers practice subject-verb agreement as they write. **Lesson 6** (Subject and Object): Writers try to use the proper forms of pronouns and *who/whom* as they write.	**Lesson 7** (Verb Tense): Writers make choices about verb tense as they write, and they strive to use verb endings and forms consistent with their choice. **Lesson 8** (Punctuating Dialogue): Writers learn to punctuate as needed while writing.	**Lesson 9** (Commas in Lists): Writers know how commas separate items in a list and use commas this way as we write. **Lesson 10** (Using Commas and Conjunctions): Writers know how to write longer sentences by joining complete sentences with a comma and a conjunction. We strive to vary our sentences this way when writing.
Drafting		**Lesson 1** (Ending Punctuation): Writers make choices about ending punctuation as they draft. **Lesson 2** (Paragraphing): Writers make choices about inserting paragraphs while drafting.	**Lesson 3** (Subject and Predicate): Writers write complete sentences as they draft. **Lesson 4** (Fragments): Writers consider their genre and audience and make decisions about fragments as they draft.	**Lesson 5** (Subject-Verb Agreement): Writers practice subject-verb agreement as they draft. **Lesson 6** (Subject and Object): Writers try to use the proper forms of pronouns, and *who/whom* as they draft.	**Lesson 7** (Verb Tense): Writers make choices about verb tense as they draft and they try to maintain verb endings consistent with their tense choice. **Lesson 8** (Punctuating Dialogue): Writers learn to punctuate dialogue properly, and we punctuate as needed while drafting.	**Lesson 9** (Commas in Lists): Writers learn how commas separate items in a list and use commas this way as we draft. **Lesson 10** (Using Commas and Conjunctions): Writers learn to write longer sentences by joining complete sentences with a comma and a conjunction. We can vary our sentences this way while drafting.	**Lesson 11** (Apostrophes): Writers understand how apostrophes signify possessive forms and contractions, and we strive to use these forms to convey meaning as we draft. **Lesson 12** (Semicolons and Colons): Writers understand that the semicolon and colon can be interesting ways to join sentences. We use them these ways as we draft.

Continues

Figure 9–3 Spiral Model for Grammar Instruction (*continued*)

	Unit 1	Unit 2	Unit 3	Unit 4	Unit 5	Unit 6	Unit 7
Revision	**Lesson 1** (End Punctuation): Writers make choices about ending punctuation as a revision strategy. **Lesson 2** (Paragraphing): Writers break their writing into smaller chunks during revision.	**Lesson 3** (Subject and Predicate): Writers compose complete sentences by including a subject and predicate. We revise our sentences. **Lesson 4** (Fragments): Writers understand that a fragment is not a sentence. We consider the appropriateness and effectiveness of fragments in revision.	**Lesson 5** (Subject-Verb Agreement): Writers revise their writing so that subject and verb agree, and we learn singular and plural forms of nouns, pronouns, and verbs to do this. **Lesson 6** (Subject and Object): Writers understand subject and object in order to use the proper form of pronouns and *who/whom*. We revise our writing to use proper forms of pronouns and *who/whom*. We revise our writing to use proper forms.	**Lesson 7** (Verb Tense): Writers make choices about verb tense as a revision strategy and they maintain the tense of their choice by learning and checking their verb endings. **Lesson 8** (Punctuating Dialogue): Writers learn to punctuate dialogue properly, and we punctuate as needed in revision.	**Lesson 9** (Commas in Lists): Writers learn how commas separate items in a list, and we revise our writing to include them. **Lesson 10** (Using Commas and Conjunctions): Writers learn to write longer sentences by joining complete sentences with a comma and a conjunction. We can revise our writing for greater sentence variety.	**Lesson 11** (Apostrophes): Writers study how apostrophes signify possessive forms and contractions, and we revise our writing to use these forms to convey meaning. **Lesson 12** (Semicolons and Colons): Writers learn that the semicolon and colon can be interesting ways to join sentences. We study their usage and try them in revision.	

From *The Power of Grammar* by Mary Ehrenworth and Vicki Vinton (2005)

Another option is to look across your writing units in a year and then compare those to the grammar skills you plan to teach. Which units tend to lend themselves to what? For example, if you have two narrative units in your year, those are likely the ones where it makes the most sense to teach quotation marks and other dialogue punctuation. If you are planning to teach different forms of paragraphing, you might teach that once in your literary essay unit, another time in your informational unit, and a third time in your fiction unit, but leave it out of your poetry unit. Still other teachers I know pick one or two skills that students will be introduced to early in a unit, and then get repeated teaching and practice throughout the unit, with the goal that students will have mastered the concept by the end of the six or seven weeks the unit takes to complete. The students then use a checklist to make sure they correctly used the skills taught in this unit, as well as the ones from previous units.

No matter what you decide to do in weaving your grammar and conventions instruction throughout your units, a few things might help to make this work more successful. Those include:

- Ensuring that students have repeated exposure to each grammar or conventions skill.

- Paying close attention to gradual release of responsibility. It's important that students see us model first, then try something alongside us and practice with their peers before they are expected to work on it independently.

- Making sure that students are able to apply what you're teaching right away and often so that it feels purposeful and they have immediate practice.

Of course, simply planning for units is not enough. There is the actual practice of teaching to consider. It helps a lot to consider how to make the teaching of grammar as engaging as possible. I like to use funny, strange, or shocking examples in my writing that are greatly affected by my grammar choices so that students are entertained, while also getting a sense of just how high the stakes are for grammar usage.

"When looking at endpoints I want to make sure the endpoint matches what I want my sentence to really say. So this sentence here:

You have eaten a cockroach.

"It seems as if I'm just stating gruesome facts with no idea about the consequences. But by adding an exclamation point:

You have eaten a cockroach!

"The reader gets a strong sense of urgency, perhaps even disgust. And if I choose to go with the question mark:

You have eaten a cockroach?

"There's a whole change in what's going on in the sentence. I am asking a question, almost with disbelief. When you write your own sentences, you want to think about the purpose of your words."

That kind of direct teaching is engaging and also likely to stick in the students' minds. Additionally, it is crystal clear and grounded in purpose—not just grammatical correctness.

It is important to employ a variety of methods so that diverse learners can learn in different ways. You will most certainly want to *demonstrate* whatever grammar conventions you are teaching with your own writing. "So, I'm looking over my writing and I am noticing that I keep going back and forth from past to present tense. I think I need to fix that so it's not confusing to my readers. My first move then will be to choose a tense and go with it," you might say, before modeling rereading your work and making the necessary corrections. However, you will of course want to make sure you are not only demonstrating during the editing process. It is important for students to see how writers use conventional language when generating, rehearsing, drafting, and revising as well. "So, I'm just going to try that out in my notebook right now . . . I'll go ahead and indent because this is the start of a paragraph . . ." you might say. Or, "When I'm drafting an essay, I try to make sure I pay attention to the commas in a list of items. It can get confusing sometimes, so even when I'm drafting, to help me make sure I am making sense to myself I will be sure to remember those commas that go in a list." All steps of the writing process have different purposes and it's very helpful for students to see how thinking changes in different situations.

Another instructional move that is very helpful, and one that students can easily take on the road with them, is the use of *mentor texts*. Many students are familiar with mentor texts for things like craft and structure. However, students should also know that if they are looking for things like noun-verb agreement, comma placement, use of semicolon and more, opening up a text that is using those things can be a great reference point. It is such a powerful tool for kids when they know that anytime they have a grammatical issue about a genre they are trying to write, yes, they could look it up online or in a grammar book, but they could also just grab a professionally published example of the genre they are writing and skim it, looking for examples of that author using that grammatical move. If you have a text—you have a grammar mentor.

One reminder that you might want to give students is that some authors (Sandra Cisneros, Avi, e.e. cummings) do not always write in conventional ways and might not serve as good mentors if the writer is going for a conventional style. That said, thinking of texts to offer as mentors and showing ones that will excite students is crucial. If you know your students love video games and you're currently in a persuasive writing unit, you might decide to bring in video game reviews for those students, for example. If some students are all about sports and you're in the middle of an informational unit, you might bring in some copies of *Sports Illustrated for Kids.*

A third teaching method, and perhaps my favorite, is using inquiry, such as was described at the top of this section. I love setting students up to "discover" something about grammar. Typically I like to pose a question like, "Find as many different types of paragraphs as you can. Study them. Then ask yourself, why do you think this author paragraphed in this way?" After a day or a week, I ask the students to compile their results, maybe on a large piece of butcher paper or on a blank SMART board. We chart the things we noticed, comment on patterns, and look for possible conclusions we can bring into our own writing. This is a gorgeous way for students to begin to develop an understanding of "conventions" versus "rules." By engaging in inquiry, students soon figure out that there are all sorts of ways that writers write, some more common than others. This can lead to great discussions about the choices writers consciously make about using conventions and when and how to make those decisions. The one thing that makes inquiry not a method you can use every day, and also engaging, is that there is no telling what students might come up with. If you have a very particular pattern or understanding you want your students to develop, inquiry is probably not a good choice.

Another teaching method, although perhaps less compelling than the other three, is to use examples or excerpts of conventionally written pieces to explain ways that grammar can work. This is a pretty classic way to teach grammar. Most of the best books on grammar contain page after page of annotated examples. There are ways to spice this up, however. One way this can be done is to take an idea from one of my favorite grammar books, *The Deluxe Transitive Vampire.* In it, each grammar and conventions topic is illustrated with gothic, vampiric examples—many of them not appropriate for school-age children. However, you might consider thinking of what you and your students do find engaging, and craft example sentences and passages to explain otherwise dry concepts. For example, most people who know me know I am fascinated by cockroaches. If I wanted to show students the difference between simple, compound, complex, and compound complex sentences, I might do something like this:

The cockroach skittered across the floor. (Simple sentence contains a subject and a verb and tells a complete thought.)

The cockroach climbed up the bed and she didn't notice. (Compound sentence is made up of two clauses connected by a conjunction.)

After the cockroach climbed onto her pillow, it slipped into her ear. (Complex sentence is made up of an independent clause and a dependent clause.)

The girl jumped out of bed but the cockroach fell out of her ear while she was shouting and managed to get away. (Compound complex sentence is a combination of a compound sentence with a complex sentence.)

It is also probably worth noting that, when it comes to grammar and conventions instruction there should be a definite balance between whole-class, small-group, and one-on-one instruction. Many of the grammar mavens I know make the whole-class instruction revolve around the key topics that their grade is responsible for teaching. They then tap one-on-one and small-group instruction for students who might have some gaps, or for students who might be ready for more sophisticated grammatical concepts. For example, a teacher might decide that her fourth-grade class is ready to tackle compound complex sentences. So, she teaches a string of lessons over a few weeks showing students how to build sentences by weaving together compound sentences with complex sentences. The progression might look like this:

> Session One: A minilesson where teacher models how to create a compound complex sentence, using her own writing.

> Session Two: Students embark on an inquiry, for over a week, where they gather examples of compound complex sentences from their reading. They theorize why and when an author might use these.

> Session Three: Students look to mentor texts to study and emulate different ways authors can create compound complex sentences.

In the meantime, there might be a group of students who are still grappling with simple sentence construction. The teacher might meet with that small group of students using inquiry and mentor texts, as well as explicit instruction, to give lots of methods and ways to tackle this foundational concept. That progression might look like this:

> Small-group meeting one: Teacher explicitly teaches what makes a simple sentence, making sure to explicitly name the parts of speech needed. Students practice writing a few simple sentences with each other.

> Small-group meeting two: Teacher explores the role different endpoints play on changing the meaning of simple sentences. She makes sure to introduce fancier endpoints like ellipses for trailing off and dashes for interrupted sentences as an entree into more grade-level sophistication.

> Small-group meeting three: Students learn how to mentor themselves to professional writers by studying a few teacher-curated texts with good examples of simple sentences, such as Donald Crews, Mo Willems, or Margie Palatini.

> Small-group meeting four: Students work in partnerships to plan seminars to teach students in younger grades about simple sentences. Students might use posters, mentor texts, or their own writing as tools.

For a couple of the more grammatically sophisticated students, she might plan a few partnership sessions where the students study different ways to play with sentence combining and shortening.

> Partner meeting one: The teacher discusses the different types of sentences and sentence lengths. She models studying her own writing to notice her patterns, then coding her own sentences. Students then help each other notice sentence patterns in their own writing.

> Partner meeting two: The teacher discusses the ways that sentence length can be connected to meaning. She has the students work on an inquiry to note hot spots in texts they've read and then to notice the sentence structure within those sections. Students notice patterns and draw conclusions, theorizing about why authors would use certain kinds of sentences when.

> Partner meeting three: Partners work together, with the teacher coaching, to look at places in their current drafts where different types of sentences can underline meaning. They can notice the difference between conjunctions, punctuation, and other ways writers build sentences, then apply these to their own writing.

To me, the most important idea about good grammar instruction that sticks is that students need to know when and why they would want to use a particular type of grammar. You might want to tap into Lisa Delpit's work and consider discussing the value of code-switching. You might want to talk about how the choices a writer makes grammatically have a direct effect on their clarity as well as their readers' interpretations. I try to share my grammar nerd credentials with my students, plainly reveling in the power of "being in charge of the way readers read" by simple choices of commas, colons, and verb endings. The more excited I am about the dizzying power of grammar, the more likely my students will also get the fever. But as soon as I veer off of that track and into the track of "rightness" and "wrongness" and "carelessness" I have already begun to lose them, while also losing whatever purposefulness I might have had in this area of instruction.

I think perhaps my final suggestion to help you along with grammar instruction in the writing workshop is for you to continue to grow in your own grammar and conventions knowledge. What is great and horrible about the English language is that it is constantly evolving. Hard-and-fast rules from when I was a child (you must always leave two spaces after an endpoint) are no longer true. Other expectations are slowly changing. (Had you heard that using "they" not only as a plural pronoun, but also as a gender-nonspecific pronoun is gaining traction?) It behooves us teachers of writing to keep up to date on the latest thinking around standard accepted language. Knowing that people have been complaining about the decline of grammar since the Venerable Bede in the eighth century helps me sleep at night. Nothing that is happening in language now is anything that hasn't happened since humans have been speaking.

With that in mind, I try very hard not to speak with children about grammar and conventions rules. I prefer to call them what linguist Sandra Wilde calls them—patterns. That way, the first time a student sees a professionally published book with a sentence that starts with *and*, I can talk about how different patterns apply to different audiences and for different purposes. I also make a point of bringing in articles and examples of interesting grammar and conventions to constantly fuel our conversations and remind students that grammar is very much alive and well. I also try to regularly read new grammar books or visit grammar blogs and websites. Some of my favorites include:

For general grammar knowledge:
Grammar Girl: www.quickanddirtytips.com/grammar-girl
The Deluxe Transitive Vampire by Karen Gordon
A Dash of Style by Noah Lukeman
Woe Is I by Patricia O'Conner

For grammar instruction:
The Power of Grammar by Mary Ehrenworth and Vicki Vinton
Practical Punctuation by Daniel Feigelson
Catching Up on Conventions by Chantal Francois and Elisa Zonana
Grammar to Enrich and Enhance Writing by Constance Weaver

✳ Ongoing Work: Grammar and Conventions Instruction Is Yearlong

I work fairly regularly with teachers in their schools on developing their grammar instruction. One teacher responded after I described what I just wrote about above with, "It is all very simple. But it is not easy to do." I would have to agree with that notion. None of the things I've tried to describe in this chapter is hard to conceptualize. However, the actual boot-on-the-ground aspects of it can be complicated. That's why I very highly recommend that you work with a committee or just a grammar-devoted group of educators to help build consensus and carry the load. If you are trying to teach grammar all by yourself in your building, it will definitely be an uphill journey. Your students won't have much to build on and not many places to go after you. (See Figure 9–4.)

Additionally I would give a full reality check: all your students' grammar needs will not be filled after just one lesson on a topic. Or several lessons. Grammar, like healthy eating and exercise, needs to be studied and practiced constantly because brains and language are constantly evolving and growing. Additionally, it is unlikely that after you and your building commit to the work, it will be completely handled. The first year or two will be tough. The first year in particular will be a bit dicey. Until every grade has had a chance to get their own topics well in hand, each grade after them will have to balance a little catch-up with the new topics for that grade level. But, working as a team, with the big goal of having grammar-savvy students, will go a long way toward gaining traction and consistency across your building.

Figure 9–4 One Way a First Year of Grammar and Conventions Curriculum Could Go

	3rd	4th	5th
Introduce	• Paragraphing • Correcting run-on sentences • Past and present tense	• Compound and complex sentences • Noun-verb agreement	• Compound-complex sentences • Using semicolons • Dependent and independent clauses • Punctuation inside of quotation marks in dialogue
Practice	• Paragraphing • Simple and compound sentences • Quotations and commas in dialogue • Commas in addresses • Pronoun antecedents • Endpoints (periods, exclamation points, question marks)	• Paragraphing • Quotations and commas in dialogue • Pronoun antecedents • Correcting run-on sentences • Noun-verb agreement • Past and present tense	• Pronoun antecedents • Correcting run-on sentences • Past and present tense • Noun-verb agreement • Paragraphing • Dependent and independent clauses • Punctuation inside of quotation marks in dialogue
Master	• Simple and compound sentences • Commas in addresses • Endpoints (periods, exclamation points, question marks)	• Paragraphing • Quotations and commas in dialogue	• Pronoun antecedents • Paragraphing • Correcting run-on sentences

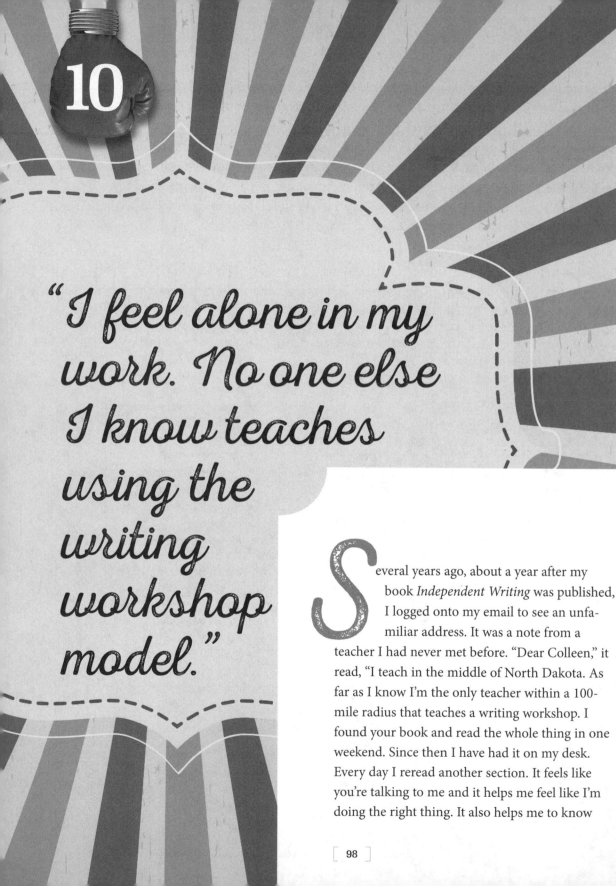

10

"I feel alone in my work. No one else I know teaches using the writing workshop model."

Several years ago, about a year after my book *Independent Writing* was published, I logged onto my email to see an unfamiliar address. It was a note from a teacher I had never met before. "Dear Colleen," it read, "I teach in the middle of North Dakota. As far as I know I'm the only teacher within a 100-mile radius that teaches a writing workshop. I found your book and read the whole thing in one weekend. Since then I have had it on my desk. Every day I reread another section. It feels like you're talking to me and it helps me feel like I'm doing the right thing. It also helps me to know that I'm not alone. That there are many teachers out there doing this work, even if I don't know them personally."

Now, the point of sharing the story isn't to be —*hey, I'm so great! My books make people feel less alone.* Although I can see how it could be read that way. Yes, I was humbled by the fact that a teacher found her way to something I wrote and it made her life just a little bit easier. But, more importantly, it reminded me of something I can sometimes forget in the community where I live and work. Namely that there are teachers in the world who feel very alone.

Whether it's deep in rural America, or else smack dab in an urban center, surrounded by hundreds of teachers who have different teaching philosophies, or even teaching in a building that is a "workshop school" but has as many divergent interpretations of that term as there are people in the building, there is a way in which, of all the troubles dealt with in this book, the solitude of teaching can be the one most likely to break the spirit of the most dedicated teacher.

✳ What Stops Us: Most of Us Need Others in Order to Grow

There are many different reasons why a teacher might find herself feeling alone. But, if you're an introvert, like me, that doesn't always have to be a problem. It's entirely possible that you may prefer to be a lone wolf. In that case, I suppose you wouldn't be reading this chapter. But for those of us who do better knowing that there are at least like-minded souls nearby, even if we don't always hang out with them, it can be incredibly challenging.

Perhaps one of the most regular challenges is when there's no one to bounce ideas off of. All of us have teaching ideas we think might be brilliant, or at least interesting, but it helps a lot to have another set of eyes to look them over with us before we test them out on the students. Does this latest strategy for addressing paragraphing sound crazy? Should I use this mentor text? Does my rubric look inviting or intimidating? The questions we might have, the ideas we might want another look at, are endless, and a quick trip down the hall to share those things can be invaluable.

Aside from simply a sounding board, it is critical to have someone to study with. As we well know from our own students, learners should learn in the company of others. No one needs to keep an active learning life more than an educator. Teaching is a lifelong learning journey, and teachers who are in it for the long haul often talk about the value of learning from and alongside other teachers. There has been a fair amount of research into the connections between teacher collaboration and student achievement. If schools want students to perform well, one of the best things they can do is support teacher collaboration. However, for more of us than we would care to admit, finding someone to collaborate with can be challenging, making it difficult for us to outgrow our own best thinking.

Perhaps not as important as student achievement, but certainly something that affects our morale, is when there's no one to complain to. This can be hard if we're alone, or if the colleagues we do have feel like they might be hostile to the work we're trying to do. When we struggle, we want to have a place to itch and moan, but then not feel as if people will misinterpret us to think we no longer believe in teaching writing the way we do. It's sort of similar to that feeling of wanting to complain about our parents to our siblings, but if anyone outside of the family complains about our folks, we get very defensive.

On the other side of that coin is that we also want others to celebrate our successes with us. Lucy Calkins has spoken about how teaching can be a lonely profession. But not always for the reasons we think. She said that when we do something amazing, like motivate a student, or teach a powerful lesson, it can be like shooting a hole-in-one and no one is watching. Sure, the students are watching, but they have no perspective, and we probably wouldn't want them to. We do something fantastic, or simply just good, and then we look up and see there is no one around to share it with. True, many of us could call a friend or a spouse, but as much as we love those people, it is only really another teacher who can truly understand what we accomplished. A few teachers have told me they would thrive and stay in this profession if there was a colleague who would bust out the bubbly with them whenever they had a teaching triumph.

✳ See Opportunity: Develop a New Kind of Community

Of course, there are plenty of reasons why being alone, or at least feeling alone, can be viewed as positive.

- *Autonomy*. With no one to share ideas with, there is no one you need to compromise for. You can design units, create tools, and teach in any way that you and your administrator see fit.

- *Clarity*. When you are working by yourself, you can keep yourself unmuddied. There are fewer distractions from your goals.

- *Time*. The only time you need to set aside is the time you need to work with your students, to learn what you want to learn, and to plan ways to use what you learn. There are no additional planning meetings to suffer through, no one else's student work to read. You can use the time you have as you see fit.

But of course, despite those positives, you might still feel as if the herculean task of working by yourself can make you feel as if you should either join the crowd and give up your vision or else leave the profession entirely. While understandable, those are not the only options. It's important to remember that facing current working conditions and our relationships with colleagues can make a huge difference in our day-to-day teaching lives.

First off, teachers are models for our students. When they see us collaborating or hear stories about our collaboration, they gain a model of what collaboration can look like and how it can affect professional life. They see how professional conversation goes between adults. They witness firsthand how interdependence can go. When they watch us sharing laughs as well as sharing staplers and understand that even though they only have their assigned teachers in their classrooms, in many ways the other teachers in the building are affecting student learning as well. When we develop collaborative relationships with colleagues, we are modeling for students how important it is to support and be supportive of others and to allow that support to seep into the rest of the community.

Our colleagues likely want or need collaboration as much as we do. Yet, aside from a few social mixers spread throughout the year, often organized by the administration or by the social community, very little attention is paid to the role of collaboration in schools. By turning your attention to it, this is an opportunity to bring others on board. It is very likely that most communities will welcome the conscious decision to work on collaboration across the school day, not just with regard to writing.

✳ Experiment: Develop, Create, or Find Learning Partners

The first thing you'll want to do is decide which path you want to take. Do you want to step fully into the role of Lone Ranger, Teacher-Who-Teaches-Workshop-All-by-Herself? This might be a very sound choice if:

- You're an introvert

- You prefer not to share ideas

- You prefer not to have your own vision of your work clouded by others

- You are too busy/overwhelmed to make time for working with other teachers

- You work in a one-room schoolhouse, with no Internet connection, spotty phone service, and very unreliable mail delivery.

Perhaps I was teasing just a bit on the last one. But the other points are possible, and are presented without judgment. I am an introvert myself. I have gone through phases where it was just so much easier to work by myself. Or at least not have to think too much about other adults while getting my teaching ducks in a row. And I do believe that for many of us this can come in phases. That said, for the many times that we would prefer to work with others,

I have a few possible tips to consider if you find that you are very alone in your writing workshop instruction.

You might begin by investigating why your colleagues do not seem to be interested in the same work you are interested in. Could it be that they had bad experiences with staff development in the past? Might they be concerned that the teaching model they have been using for years may be at risk? Are they simply not passionate about writing? Has there been a lot of pressure by administrators for teachers to try the work, and so teachers look at people who are practicing it as somehow turncoat? Depending on what you discover, finding out why people in your building are not supporting the work is likely the first step in solving this problem. Know that this can happen casually during Friday Happy Hour or during a more formal grade meeting. It really depends on the culture of your school and when people are more likely to feel comfortable enough to be honest. You might want to be prepared for the worst-case scenario, just so that you have your game face already picked out.

MAKE A LEARNING BUDDY

No matter how that conversation goes, or even if you decide to never have it, it is still a good idea to try to get a buddy in your school. Sometimes there are people who can become that one colleague we really need, we just have to find ways of connecting with them. Often people have very good reasons for not wanting to teach writing in the ways you and I deeply believe in. Sometimes they actually haven't thought that much about it. Rather than just assume that there is no way we could get anyone on our sides, we can try to bring them over to the dark side. One of the ways I find works well is to share student work in a nonbragging way. Not that I really have to tell you not to brag. I find that most teachers are the absolute worst at bragging. We don't even brag when we completely should. That said, often when we see something our students do that is amazing we hesitate to share. But sharing our students' work is often one of the best ways to allow colleagues to see what your students can do, without saying "Look how great I am!" Most teachers love to celebrate student achievements with other teachers.

If that feels too vulnerable, you might consider finding someone with complementary but different skill sets. Maybe there's a colleague who is a master of mathematics, or perhaps the perfect bulletin board designer, or teaches spelling in compelling ways. Try linking up with this person by asking to learn from them. Be honest. Find a colleague who you think is someone you might like to get to know better or who might be interested in what you do. Oftentimes people are glad to be just spoken to plainly. While you are learning from them you are also opening a door for them to want to learn with you.

You might also consider inviting people into your classroom (or ask to visit theirs). If you're feeling brave, sometimes hanging up a sign over the time clock, or sending an email to the staff asking people if they'd like to come to your room (for a celebration, a new use of technology, a cool strategy you're going to try) or if you can visit theirs can build bridges between colleagues. Teachers love to visit each other's classrooms, and we also love to be visited. Yet, it can be entrenched in school communities to stay in our own rooms with the doors shut. Sometimes all it takes is an invite to build that bridge, which can lead to lots more visits and conversations.

Of course, if those strategies feel vulnerable, you might consider starting a professional book club within your school. Ask your principal to pay for a few copies of a professional text or else ask people to find their own copies. Then set up some times to meet to discuss the book. This can give a great entrée to people who might be curious about the work, but haven't yet figured out a way to learn about it. Also — people love free stuff!

FIND A COMMUNITY OUTSIDE OF YOUR SCHOOL

Maybe making a new buddy just isn't possible for you. This can be the case for people who teach in a very small school or one deeply entrenched in a particular method of instruction. Finding a community outside of your school community can be a good option. There are a few easy ways to do this. One way is to attend regional or district training focused on writing or related topics. The training can be focused on the type of writing instruction you value — but it might not be. It never hurts to hear another perspective. When you attend these, keep your ears open for like-minded souls. Since these people are geographically accessible, you can not only set up times to meet up for coffee or to visit bookstores, but ideally also times to visit each other in your respective schools. Getting a chance to visit a new site and see a colleague you respect teach (or having him visit you) can be exactly the breath of fresh air that you need.

You might also consider attending a national conference that focuses on writing, or the broader topic of literacy. Two great organizations (and strong options to consider) include the National Council of Teachers of English (NCTE), which has its annual conference every November, and the International Reading Association (IRA), which has its annual conference in July. There are frequently roundtable discussions and plenty of other opportunities to meet with educators from around the country. Often there are regional discussions that allow people to connect with people located close to them.

Another option is to consider attending institutes and retreats on the topic of writing instruction. In these you might opt for ones that share philosophies and ideals similar to the ones you have. The Teachers College Reading and Writing Project, which is the organization I work with, runs two a year in New York City. Additionally there are other well-known annual institutes and retreats, including the Boothbay Literacy Retreat and Growing Educators, to name a couple. At institutes such as these I have made lifelong friends who have helped support my own professional development over the years. Be sure to exchange emails and contact information so that you can keep the relationship going long after your week together is over.

If you are geographically isolated or strapped for cash or time or simply not a fan of face-to-face interactions with adults, you might find virtual communities more to your taste. If the one you are hoping for is not there, you can create one. There is certainly no substitute for face-to-face interactions with people. But sometimes, because of time constraints, budget, or just simply a tendency toward introversion, this just isn't possible. Luckily, the twenty-first century has made it easier than ever through social networking, online courses, webinars, and the like, to create virtual professional learning networks. Following are a few suggestions, organized from easiest to most complicated (knowing that these were the most up-to-date suggestions at the time this book was published):

- Sign up for an online course or webinar. These are probably the easiest entrée into the world of digital community because these opportunities offer a platform that is fairly familiar (a seminar, a class), but using digital tools. They often offer tutorials and other forms of support to participants. Most of the best offer opportunities to interact with other participants (see appendix for suggestions).

- Join Twitter, Facebook, LinkedIn, or another social media network. My favorite, shockingly, is Twitter for professional connections. I was completely anti-Twitter until my friend Kate Roberts talked me into joining. Unlike Facebook, I primarily use Twitter to connect with other educators and writers. I have "attended" Twitter chats, learned about upcoming events, and been informed of the latest research. I have also started and maintained relationships with people who I later have had the opportunity to meet in person. Many educators I work with on a daily basis say they owe a huge debt to social media for giving them the professional support they need.

- Start your own blog. Blogs are a perfect platform for sharing your successes and struggles. They are also a great way to virtually meet other educators, bloggers and nonbloggers alike. Hearing from individual classrooms is a powerful tool for transforming educational practice. Blogging is free and self-driven. So you can be as prolific as you'd like, or not.

✳ Ongoing Work: When Loneliness Rears Its Head Again

Depending on which options you choose to go with, there is certainly a possibility that they won't work out for you long term. Perhaps that colleague across the hall transferred to another school. Perhaps that webinar you signed up for was less than helpful. Maybe the friends you made at the annual convention got too busy with their own lives and you drifted apart. No matter what happened, it is possible that you might find yourself back at the starting line again. While it can be disheartening to have this happen, it can help to keep a few things in mind:

- You are not actually alone. There are thousands of us out here who believe what you believe when it comes to the teaching and learning of writing.

- You can always start again with the suggestions above. Maybe move down the list and try options that you did not try before.

- Depending on the circumstance, it might be time to try something more drastic. For example, more than one teacher I know has decided to quit her current job and move to a school or community that shares the same goals and beliefs. Sometimes this is as simple as applying to work in a school the next town over. Sometimes this means uprooting entirely and moving across the country.

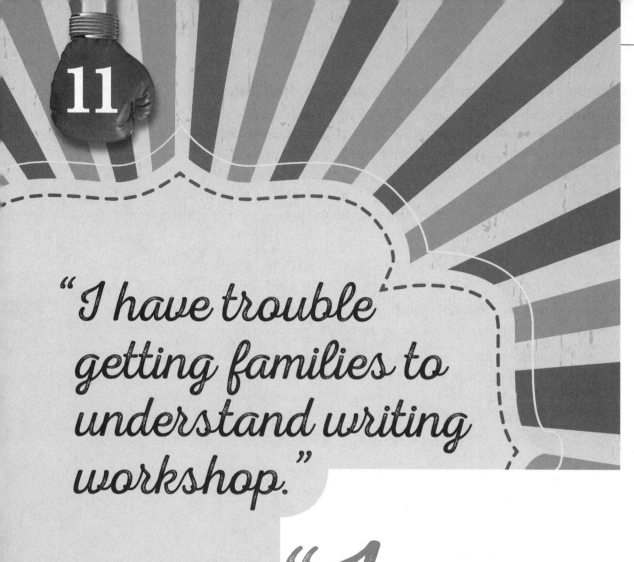

11

"I have trouble getting families to understand writing workshop."

"It's all well and good that students are learning to 'find their voices,' but my child tells me that you don't think spelling or grammar counts."

"I love to write. Can I come in and help during writing workshop?"

"How can you be teaching essays when my kid can't even write a sentence?"

"There's too much homework, so I tell him he doesn't need to do his writing homework. He just needs to do the things that count—like math or reading. Is that okay?"

"I just don't get this whole writing workshop thing. I don't know how to help her."

I've heard all of the above comments during parent/teacher conferences, curriculum nights, and open houses. I've heard the whole gamut, from things that would make your hair curl, to things that would warm the cockles of your darkest pessimistic heart. I'm assuming that at least one thing above sounds familiar to you. No matter how heart-warming or hair-curling these things are, I tend to believe that every caregiver wants what's best for their child's education. So whether they completely buy into the work you're trying to do in writing workshop or whether they are skeptical, the reason they are those things is because of their desire for the best. It is also important to remember that research shows that the more involved a child's family is in her education, the more successful that child's education will be. It is therefore one of our most important jobs to educate families about writing workshop and recruit them to be part of our team.

✳ What Stops Us: There Is as Much Diversity In Families as There Is in Our Kids

One of the funny things about being a teacher is that because everyone went to school they feel as if they know exactly how it goes in all classrooms. But, unless you are very young or you went to a very progressive school as a child, the chances are strong that the way you learned about writing is very different than the way you teach writing to your students. It can be helpful to remember that it is also likely very different from the way the grownups in your students' lives learned about writing. What this means is that, while it is important to communicate with families about all areas of the curriculum, it is especially important to communicate with them about areas that you know will be different from their personal experiences and (perhaps) their expectations for the subject.

And, of course, no matter what the topic is, communication that is about the connections and disconnections between expectations and realities can be tricky. Add to the mix that you are likely to have as much diversity in your grownups as you do in your students, and things can get very tough, very quickly.

Perhaps the families I hear teachers share the most concerns about are the families who are not involved. There are many reasons why the grownups in our students' lives might not show up to school conferences or answer emails. There are work obligations, other children to tend to, life stresses, cultural differences, personal issues . . . The list of possibilities goes on and on. The first step for me is, rather than try to figure out why a family is not as involved as I would like, is to believe that all families care about their children. Some are able to show that care through school support and involvement. Others are not. But, believing that all families do care about their children can sometimes ease the difficulty of having grownups that we rarely, if ever, communicate with. That said, not knowing what the family at home thinks and whether or not they are able to support their students with writing can make communicating with them a little bit like feeling around in the dark.

On the other end of the spectrum are families who are very involved. This presents its own kind of challenges. We see them at drop-off and pick-up. We see their emails nightly in our inboxes. They are a constant presence at every school event. This can be a great thing. But it can also be a tough thing — especially if we feel like we still want to get our sea legs under us for the school year, and feel like every time we see them we should have more information than we have.

Or, sometimes, perhaps even more challenging, is the family that is not particularly supportive (yet) of the way we teach writing. To be honest, not many grownups have firm educational philosophies about the best practices for writing instruction. Sometimes though, you will get one. Or six. These folks are often teachers. They could be professional writers or editors. Perhaps they're big believers in "correctness" above all. No matter what the difference is, or why they differ, it can be very challenging to communicate with all of your class families when you know the families who disagree with you are there in the mix.

There can also be difficulties when we have families we admire, strange as that may sound. In my time as a classroom teacher I had one parent who won an NEA grant for poetry. Two others were editors for major publishing houses and countless others were just great all-around people. As embarrassing as this is to admit, I wanted them to like my pedagogy. I wanted them to hear about our curriculum and think, "That's fantastic!" Sometimes thinking about them and planning to communicate with them was more nerve-wracking than I cared to admit.

And sometimes what stops us has nothing to do with particular families and their relationships with school, but rather the peculiar nature of writing workshop and how personal it can get very quickly. Students often write stories, essays, and informational books about their lives. Sometimes these pieces of writing can venture into sensitive territory for families. This can sometimes be comical, or even embarrassing for families. An episode of the sitcom from several years ago, *Everybody Loves Raymond* (Season 6, episode 1, "The Angry Family"), deals with just this issue when one of the children shares a writing piece at a crowded school writing celebration, which describes a family as angry. While a very funny episode, especially if you either know writing workshop or have children, one can well imagine how a real family might feel in a similar situation. Sometimes the things students share about their families go beyond merely embarrassing and can tread into more serious territory. Because of this, for some classrooms and some students, writing workshop can be tricky for families. Some teachers have reported that students share that their families don't want them to share certain things in school. "Mom told me not to write about that," a child might say. Walking the tightrope between honoring a child's right to tell his own truths and a family's right to privacy can be a tricky one.

All of these concerns about communication with families can be compounded by pressure from administration. There are endless numbers of ways that communication with families can be made tougher by your administration. If your administration doesn't believe in the work, but is "letting you try it," you might feel that having the parents on your side is of paramount importance. If the administration is for the work, you might worry that what you are saying does not match entirely with the school's philosophy. Perhaps there is even conflict across the administration as to the best ways to communicate with families. Whatever it is, the tough stuff about communication does not only involve the families.

✳ See Opportunity: Families Are Crucial to Student Success

One of my fondest memories from high school was the day after parent-teacher conferences. I was a sophomore. I remember being so embarrassed by the fact that *both* my parents insisted on going to the conferences with each of my teachers. Most of my friends' parents had long ago stopped going. But, when I got to my first-period art class, I was surprised by what I saw at my seat: two pen-and-ink sketches of the Ramones, my favorite band. One by my dad, one by my mom. They were very different, but also, surprisingly, very good. My art teacher had asked each parent to draw something that their kid liked.

As I quickly slipped the drawings into a folder, I noticed a few other students with similar drawings. For just a brief moment I felt my parents' presence in my classroom, as well as feeling as if they really saw me at home. The simple act of having them involved, if even just a little, in my education, cracked through my adolescent armor and made me pay attention a little more in art class, and smile a little more easily at home. The power of the home-school connection cannot be overstated.

Whether we want them to be or not, there will be some families, if not a whole bunch of them, who will want to be part of our school days. As was mentioned above, writing is one of the most personal subjects we are likely to teach, so it stands to reason that parents and other caregivers can't help but be involved.

And, we all know families should be involved whenever possible. This was mentioned earlier, but it is worth restating: research shows that students whose families are involved in their schooling are more likely to be successful students. The better we can communicate with them and set parameters for our work with them, the better it will be for everyone involved.

Depending on where you stand in your community with writing workshop — one of the many, the only one, or somewhere in between — it helps to have people who believe in what you do. Most families, even the ones who do not believe in workshop to begin with, will eventually find much to admire. Having families being the biggest supporters of the work makes everything much easier.

This is because families can be great co-teachers, or even co-conspirators. If families believe in the work, they are more likely to share stories with their kids, ask questions instead of tell ideas, perhaps even carve out a writing space for their young authors in the living room. We can make it possible for students to see the connections between what their teachers want from them and their families.

When students see that we are in regular and open communication with their families, they are witnessing healthy collaborative educational relationships — the kind we would like them to foster in the future with other teachers, and if they happen to raise kids of their own someday, the kind of relationship they will foster with them.

❋ Experiment: Proactive Communication

Teachers who have the healthiest relationships with families have almost invariably actively sought those relationships out. There is very little that is accidental when home and school relationships are mutually supportive and beneficial. There are several things teachers and schools tend to do to help cultivate those relationships.

First and foremost, you will likely want to enlist the administration or your grade team to join you on this journey. It is wonderful, no matter where you teach, for the school, or at least grade-level teams, to speak with one voice regarding curriculum. That said, it is especially vital when communities are new or perhaps even hostile to the work. Without a clear and unified vision, lots of misconceptions can form that can lead to trouble. If at all possible, ask your administrator, or co-write alongside your colleagues, a description of what writing workshop looks like in your community. Either include this letter in the school handbook, the handouts for back to school night, or some other can't-miss spot. If, for whatever reason, you cannot enlist administrators or colleagues to work together on a joint communication to families, you can always do one yourself. You can explain a few crucial things families can do to support their students at home in each subject area and what key curricular goals you might have. (See Figure 11–1.)

In addition to letters, you might consider preparing to talk or write about writing regularly with a few key points. By being prepared for possible questions or issues you are less likely to be caught flat-footed when confronted with tricky conversations. One of the biggest fears I had when I was in the classroom was dealing with conflicts with parents and caregivers. I hate conflicts. My partner gave me the best advice with regard to this: have some one-liners in your pocket, just as politicians, actors, and athletes do for interviews.

Figure 11-1 Family Letter

Dear Families,

Thank you so much for sharing your children with our classroom this year! We are only a few days into the school year and I can already tell that this is going to be a year filled with learning and fun.

Soon we will have our curriculum night, where I will speak with you in more detail about the curriculum. But I know that several of you have had questions regarding the way we teach writing in our classroom. I thought I would send this letter to give you an initial introduction to the methods we use and also a few tips you can try if you want to support your child at home.

First off, in our classroom we teach using the writing workshop model. This is a decades-old model that has years of research in classrooms across the world. It is based on the authentic process writers go through when they write a piece for publication. This process develops and becomes more independent as children get older. If your child was in a writing workshop classroom when he or she was younger you will see some things that are familiar and some things that are different.

Typically we have students collect ideas, experiment, and develop ideas in their writer's notebooks. These are the notebooks that you see coming to and from home and school on a daily basis. We encourage students to write in them every day, for a few minutes at least, in order to continually collect possible material for future pieces. You might notice that the work in the notebook can sometimes be a little disjointed, messy, sometimes unfinished; other times it reads like a fully developed piece. That's okay. The notebook is a place where students generate ideas, and not all ideas will require the same kind of attention.

After students have chosen an idea, they will then move on to drafting their pieces onto paper outside of the notebook or on their computers. We try to go through that step in the process quickly so that students have plenty of time to revise. When students revise, they are working on big-ticket changes in order to make sure their meaning shines — refining structure, writing new beginnings, elaborating on key points. From there, students will work on editing, which means they will be doing final checks on spelling, punctuation, and other conventions. Although, to be fair, we do ask students to edit as they go through the entire process, but many students need that final check in case they missed something.

When a piece has worked its way through the process, students might choose to publish it — that is, make it ready for readers. Sometimes this involves typing the piece up, sometimes this involves copying it over, other times it means crafting an attractive cover. We then take a bit of time to celebrate.

The thing we focus on most in writing workshop is improving the writer's skills as a writer. While we value the final piece, it's not the final product that we are most interested in, but rather how the writer grew and changed over the process.

Most of the direct teaching of writing workshop happens in school. But if you would like to support your young writer at home, here are a few possible ideas:

- Storytell whenever you can. While driving in the car or around the dinner table, share stories from your day or your past and encourage your child to do the same.

- Create a writing space for your child. This can be a desk, a cozy corner, or a hiding place under the table with a flashlight. You might want to set your child up with paper, a few pens, and other tools to complete the space.

- Read to your child every day. Read anything. Newspaper articles, emails from Grandma, novels. Sometimes as children get older and can read for themselves we pull back on reading aloud to them. But, children can gain a felt sense of various genres by being read to, as well as develop a love of language.

- Share your own writing process with your child. If you write anything, whether an email or an assignment for work or a project for the family, share how you went about creating that piece of writing — both the struggles and the successes.

- When your child is writing, try to only give quick bits of help. Asking questions or limiting yourself to just a sentence or two can help a student get the support they need while also fostering independence. Some questions or comments you might use include:

    - What are you hoping your reader will get from this piece?

    - What's your favorite part?

    - What strategies have you used? Show me where you used them.

    - Your writing reminds me of _____ (insert favorite author's name) because _____.

    - You worked very hard on this. I can tell that you _____.

Please let me know if you have any questions or comments you'd like to make about our class's writing curriculum. I look forward to seeing you on curriculum night!

Me

I took some time at the beginning of each school year to sit down and write down all the anticipated questions, comments, and concerns families might have. Then I thought through possible answers. That way, the next time a parent said, "Why doesn't spelling count?" instead of stumbling over my words I could respond well with my prepared comments. "Well, actually spelling counts quite a bit. We actively teach spelling in this school, focusing on students' developmental readiness to approach different spelling challenges. We hold students accountable for the words we know and expect that they can spell. The ones they are not developmentally ready for we encourage them to think through and use strategies, but not let them get in the way of other aspects of writing that they are prepared for." (See Figure 11–2.)

Figure 11–2 Common Questions and Comments Families Ask and Possible Responses

Family Question or Comment:	Possible Response:
When are you planning to work on grammar? I haven't seen anything yet.	"I'm so glad you asked that! As you know, we use the latest research to help us make our curricular decisions in our school. And the latest research shows us that grammar is best taught integrated into practice, as opposed to isolated. So, approximately 20 percent of my writing instruction is dedicated to grammar. I follow our school/district's scope and sequence, as well as state standards, to decide on whole-class teaching points, while also relying on assessments of authentic writing to tailor individual teaching that is matched to each student's developmental readiness."
Why don't you read my son's writing homework? I never see any markings on any of his writing work.	"I regularly read your son's writing. Both when I am checking homework and when I am meeting with your son one-on-one. Sometimes I give him my feedback verbally. Sometimes I write it on a sticky note, which he may or may not choose to keep in his notebook."
Do you mind if I help my daughter with her writing homework? She always has so much trouble with it.	"I would love if you were able to pitch in. It can be very rewarding. I think the tricky thing can sometimes be to make sure that the student is doing most of the work, and we are just giving quick tips and encouragement. You might want to refer to my letter I sent home at the beginning of the year for some strategies for helping."
I know my son needs help with writing. But I'm not a very good writer.	"We're all learning this together. You don't need to consider yourself a good writer to help your son with his writing though. Often what he needs most is a place to write, an appreciative audience, and someone who asks questions to help him make sure his writing makes sense. None of those things require writing expertise."

Another nice way to bring families into the loop is to regularly update about class projects and deadlines. Like many of my colleagues, I sent out a monthly newsletter letting families know about topics that would be taught in class, any upcoming trips, and things they might want to do at home with their children. I made it a priority to always include the writing unit our class was currently working on, as well as the deadline for that unit. I made sure to mention if there was anything special that needed to happen at home (or not) and any important goals or expectations I might have. This newsletter had a two-pronged purpose. It kept families informed. But it also kept me honest—once I put it in the newsletter, I needed to stick to it as much as possible.

I feel that it is worth noting, no matter how you address families, orally or in writing, you will likely want to use thoughtful language so as to be as inclusive as possible. Kristin Beers, a teacher at P.S. 29 in Brooklyn, told me she makes a point of not using the term "parents," "moms & dads," or even "caregivers." She prefers to instead use a more open term, such as "families" or "grownups." When she does this she knows that students can see their own families reflected in the classroom communications and therefore more linked to the classroom community.

Another way to bring families in and make writing workshop more accessible and understandable is to host a family writing night. One of my favorite events I ever did was a high school family writing night. Grownups came to the school auditorium with their kids. Kids were asked to bring their writing notebooks. Adults were given a brand-new one at the door. I then proceeded to show sample student writing (I chose personal narrative) from their district, going up the grades. I took the adults and their kids through a speed version of the writing process, allowing them to gather ideas, rehearse one, draft and revise. I then ended with a little question-and-answer time. It was a fantastic way for the adults to get a sense of what writing workshop was like, and for their kids to help explain it. While you might not do it exactly that way, or you might be more inclined to include it as part of a curriculum night, I cannot stress enough how powerful it is for families to see student work across the grades as well as to try their own hand at writing. Also, by writing alongside their children, many families find that any of the things that were confusing, perhaps even threatening, about writing workshop, make more sense.

If you plan to assess your students on their writing, I suggest that the assessments are also accessible to the students in a kid-friendly version that they receive at the beginning of the unit. Carl Anderson has great examples of these in his book *Assessing Writers*, as does Lucy Calkins and the Reading and Writing Project in the *Units of Study for Writing* book sets. Encourage students to take these checklists home to families early and throughout the writing process so that families know from beginning to end how best to support their students. The assessments can serve as not only a window into student performance, but also your expectations.

Another great way to pull families into writing workshop is to publish in a variety of ways. This might feel like an odd place to mention publishing work, but for many parents, the primary way they see what students are learning in writing is by noticing when the published pieces come home. Clearly many pieces will simply be written on paper and published with construction-paper covers. But there are other options that can allow families a window into your teaching, including:

Class anthologies: Include a piece of every student's work in the anthology, then make copies to go home. It allows families to see the sheer variety of topics and skills in your class.

Online publishing: Using a protected website like your class web page, you can have students scan and/or type their pieces for publication. Families can not only read the pieces at home, they can also share the work with relatives and family friends. Just make sure only student first names or initials are used.

Bare Books or other keepsake-quality publication: Many teachers I work with try to make at least one published piece of heirloom quality. The reason why is that, whether we like it or not, families have limited space and a lot of our students' writing will ultimately end up lost. However, that special hand-sewn book or one made with lift-the-flaps is more likely to stick around.

Quick Response codes: Those little scannable bits you have seen in a few places in this book can be great ways for parents to access not only student work, but also student voice. Some teachers like to record students reading their pieces out loud, then save those files to a QR code which allows families to listen to it later.

Wearable publication: One of my amazing colleagues, Bonni Gordon, a fifth-grade teacher at Hartshorne Elementary School in New Jersey, had her students publish their writing on T-shirts that the students then wore to school. I could imagine all sorts of different wearable ways for students to publish their writing and bring it back and forth from home and school.

Finally, and for many of you this goes without saying, invite families to class celebrations. This is perhaps the most obvious idea to experiment with. Now, to be clear, I am not suggesting you open every celebration to families every time. I well know how much work those sorts of celebrations are. However, if you can do it once or twice a year, it can make a huge difference in building those home-school connections. Students can sit in small groups, read into a microphone, have a silent read around the room, or even change venues and read at a picnic in a park or at a local bookstore. We'll want to spend some time preparing students for these celebrations — making sure their pieces and their presentation of them are the best they can be. It can be nerve-wracking for kids (and us), but it gives students a very important audience to write for; it also reminds them that they are part of a larger community and their words matter. Opening our classrooms at least twice a year to a student-run or -planned celebration helps families to witness firsthand the power and joy of writing workshop.

✳ Ongoing Work: When They Show Up with the Pitchforks and Torches Anyway

What if, despite all your best efforts, you still have families that not only don't understand what you're doing, but it makes them angry that you are doing it? I would suggest, first and foremost, that you gauge how angry they actually are. If they are merely annoyed, you might keep trying some of the more fun options. (Have you tried a beatnik poetry celebration with bongos and berets?) But, in all seriousness, I also encourage you to ask for administrative support if things get hostile. Avoid phone conversations. Encourage email correspondence instead. Always have an administrator sitting in on face-to-face conversations.

Additionally, you might want to bear in mind that sometimes, oftentimes, the reason we are having a difficult time connecting with the adults in our students' lives has less to do with us or our students and more to do with the complicated lives of adults. Some families are hard to accommodate because they are going through a divorce. Some grownups can't schedule a phone conference because they are working two shifts to keep food on the table. Some families are embarrassed about their struggles with their own literacy, or home language or parenting style. Trying to remember that often when there are roadblocks it is not about us can help us develop a new strategy to build a relationship with a grownup who for whatever reason is disconnected from her child's classroom. We can aim to keep striving until we make contact with them all.

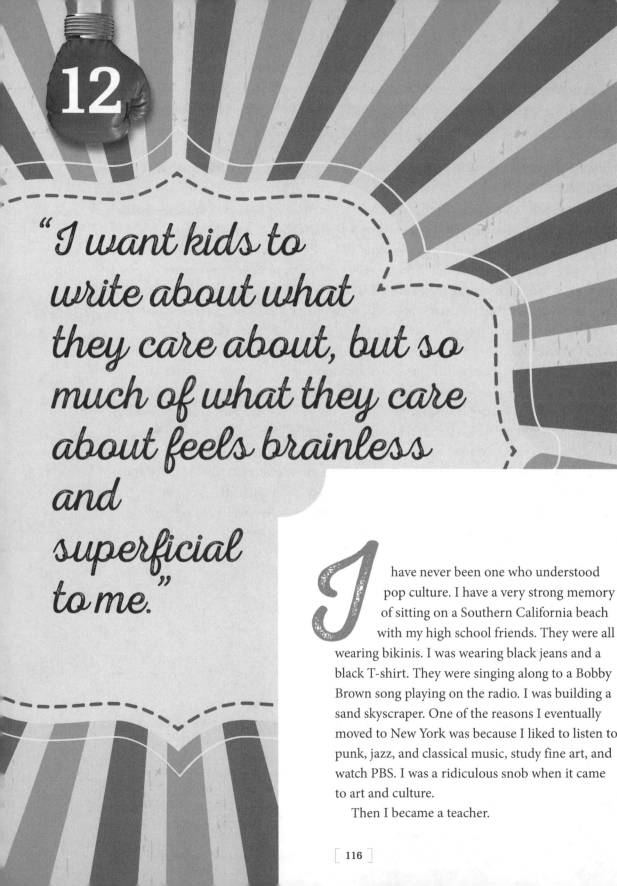

12

"*I want kids to write about what they care about, but so much of what they care about feels brainless and superficial to me.*"

I have never been one who understood pop culture. I have a very strong memory of sitting on a Southern California beach with my high school friends. They were all wearing bikinis. I was wearing black jeans and a black T-shirt. They were singing along to a Bobby Brown song playing on the radio. I was building a sand skyscraper. One of the reasons I eventually moved to New York was because I liked to listen to punk, jazz, and classical music, study fine art, and watch PBS. I was a ridiculous snob when it came to art and culture.

Then I became a teacher.

And I quickly learned that as much as ethnic, religious, and racial backgrounds play a role in students' cultures and values, so too does the dominant culture of their times. This is often comprised of things like professional sports, top forty music, video games, and social media. Student after student would turn in pieces about these things. I would read five-page stories about a basketball game someone watched on television, or a several-page essay extolling the virtues of Beyoncé.

I'm not proud to admit how I handled the situation. I simply forbade students writing anything about professional sports, pop music, television, film, or video games. "You can only write about things from your own life," I declared self-righteously. "And those things are other people's creations."

Not surprisingly, my writing workshop classroom started to go south.

✳ What Stops Us: Pop Culture Doesn't Always Reflect Our Strongest Hopes for Our Students

There are actually quite a few reasons that students' writing about these topics makes teaching writing hard. So challenging in fact, that other than questions about time, students choosing to write about topics from pop culture is one of the questions I hear most from teachers.

For one thing, when students write about these topics, they have walked into a possible minefield in terms of appropriateness for school. It used to be, back in the day, that professional sports could give you some safety net, but as athletes come more and more into the sphere of celebrity and more of their actions are captured and shared online, even that's not "safe" anymore. Some songs use curse words or talk about topics that children probably shouldn't be thinking about. Some video games have violence so graphic and realistic they can make players gasp. Do we need to even get into the fraught nature of television and movies? Most teachers want to think long and hard before actively inviting those things into the classroom, especially now that we're under more scrutiny than ever before.

Another reason we flinch in the face of pop culture is that we know so much of it doesn't sound positive for students. For example:

- American kids (aged eight to ten) spend on average eight hours a day on screen time. Teens can spend as many as eleven hours per day on screen time. (American Academy of Pediatrics, 2013)

- Black and Latino kids spend on average five more hours a day on media than their white counterparts. ("Generation M²: Media in the Lives of 80 18 Year Olds," a Kaiser Family Foundation Study, 2010)

- Pop music is more homogeneous than it was in the past with less timbral variety and pitch content. ("Is Pop Music Evolving or Just Getting Louder?" by John Matson, *Scientific American*, July 2012)

- All kids, regardless of race or socioeconomics, spend an average of thirty-eight minutes on print for pleasure per day. ("Generation M²: Media in the Live of 80 18 Year Olds," a Kaiser Family Foundation Study, 2010)

- There is a correlation between simply owning a video game console and poor academic performance. ("Gaming Frequency and Academic Performance," *Australasian Journal of Educational Technology* by Barry Ip, Gabriel Jacobs, and Alan Watkins)

Still another reason why dealing with students writing about these topics is tough has to do with the chapter before this one — students can easily hide behind these topics when they could be writing about something more important. They can turn the spotlight away from themselves and instead turn it toward someone else's story, game, or song. Since we are in the business of helping students to find their authentic voices and to use writing to help broadcast those voices, there is something particularly irksome when students choose to use that time to instead write about someone else's work. Especially work that so often feels shallow and inconsequential at best, degrading and violent at worst.

✳ See Opportunity: Embrace the Kid by Embracing Kid Culture

When I first started writing this book three years ago, the entire book was going to be about using pop culture in your classroom. Clearly it has morphed since then. That was because I was of the firm mindset that if you can't beat them, you might as well join them. In my journey to write that original book, I did a ton of research into pop culture and what I found changed me and the way I view pop culture forever.

For example, for a long time I had referred to, and had heard many other people refer to, highbrow and lowbrow culture. High culture was things like opera, fine arts, Shakespeare. And low culture was things like pop music, the Simpsons, and comic books. I was shocked to learn that the term had actually originated from Phrenology — the study of the shape of people's skulls. Those with high brows were superior and those with low brows inferior (*The Myth of Popular Culture*, by Perry Meisel, 2009). Culture was thus divided that way — some was better and therefore more worthy. Other culture was somehow worse and therefore less worthy. Perhaps even harmful.

It was then that I started thinking more about that idea. I knew that at one point the venerated Shakespeare and even opera were once popular with the lower as well as middle and upper classes. It made me begin to think that so much of what makes something pop culture has little or nothing to do with its quality or content, but rather how it holds up over time. One of my favorite quotes supporting that notion is from Stephen Sondheim: "The fact is, popular culture dates. It grows quaint. How many people feel strongly about Gilbert and Sullivan today compared to those who felt strongly in 1890?"

If we follow this argument, for all we know, if Beyoncé's popularity, her effect on the greater culture, and people's opinion of the quality of her work continue to be strong, Beyoncé might end up becoming this generation's Maria Callas. Stephen King could become this generation's Shakespeare and Minecraft could one day be held in as high esteem as chess. The only things separating them from moving from the world of popular culture into "Culture" with a capital C is the opinion of experts, and the test of time.

Once I came to the conclusion that we actually don't know which kinds of kid culture will make that move into being viewed as more respectable culture, I had to reflect a bit on my past. I started to think about what having this sort of judgmental attitude I had been carrying around for years said about me and my respect, or lack of respect, for the culture my students held dear. After all, I would never think to look down or ban from the classroom topics that had to do with their ethnic culture, for example. For many of our students, sports, video games, television, movies, and pop music form the fabric of their dominant culture. Their Super Bowl parties and television-watching marathons are just as important to them as mariachis and piñatas were to me growing up. Just as we would never tell a student that she could not write about mariachis, we might consider biting our tongues when she wants to write about whatever latest heartthrob is on the top ten. Our students need to know that we value their lives, all of what goes on in their lives, in order to feel that they can bring and share those lives with their writing in the classroom. As Randy Bomer has said, "If you will teach me, first you must love me." That includes everything.

There's also the unexpected finding that there are actually quite a few positives that come with pop culture, including:

- Playing certain complex video games has been shown to improve cognitive flexibility and strategic thinking. ("Real-Time Strategy Game Training: Emergence of Cognitive Flexibility Trait" by Brian Glass, Todd Maddow, and Bradley Love, 2013)

- People are often more productive when listening to music. ("The Effect of Music Listening on Work Performance," in *Psychology of Music* by Teresa Lesiuk, 2005)

- Television shows, even kids' shows, have more complex characters and plot lines than ever before, which requires deeper comprehension and activates more parts of our brain. (*Everything Bad Is Good for You* by Steven Johnson, 2006)

- When children play exer-games (*Just Dance, Wii Sports*) they burn four to eight times the calories they do when spending the same amount of time on the treadmill. ("Energy Cost of Exergaming: A Comparison of the Energy Cost of 6 Forms of Exergaming," *Archives of Adolescent and Pediatric Medicine*, 2011)

Then there's something else. There's the reality that part of our job as teachers is to help open the world to our students — to expose them to whole universes they might not have known existed. This includes art forms and strategies and skills across the content areas. However, many of our students are not naturally drawn to what we want to share. We say "comparative literary essays" and they say "ugh." We say "free verse poetry" and they say "meh." I find to bridge that gap, there are few things as compelling or as effective as tapping pop culture.

Pop culture can be used as a carrot to get students in the door to learn about the things we wish they would learn about. We can use the things we know our students are most passionate about to teach them the things we know they most need to know. All of a sudden pop culture is my favorite thing on the planet.

✳ Experiment: Cultural Inquiry + Instructional Connections = Big Dividends

If you're still reading, that means you haven't decided I was a crackpot and thrown the book away (or deleted it if you're reading this in e-book form). I will take that to mean that you are interested in considering the ways that pop culture can be used, as a tool to help you create the kind of writing workshop you'd like to have for your students. The first step in the process will be to get to know what your students actually like. You will want to repeat this process every year, because pop culture changes at a lightning pace, and what is cool one year can be the epitome of uncool the next year. I recommend giving out a survey. (See Figure 12–1.)

I have also found that making the survey anonymous helps let students know they can really be honest. Many students hesitate to tell the truth on these surveys when they think they will be judged badly. They know that teachers as a group don't tend to look kindly on video games and TV watching, among other things. So many of them will deny ever having even seen a video game, let alone having a favorite. Anonymity helps to combat that. By looking over the survey you can get a sense of how much media exposure your students

Figure 12–1 Student Interest Questionnaire

Please be as honest as you can. If you need more room, feel free to add more paper.

- Name: (optional)
- What's your <u>favorite</u> subject in school? Why?
- What's your <u>least</u> favorite subject in school? Why?
- What do you look forward to most in school every day? Describe it.
- What do you do after school?
- Do you play sports, dance, or do another physical activity? If so, please describe below.

- Do you read for fun (not just for homework)? If so, what are your favorite things to read?
- List your favorite television shows, or shows that you watch the most:
- How often do you watch television? (Every day, only on weekends, once day a week, every once in a while, never)
- List your favorite musicians:
- What are your favorite songs?
- Do you use a computer, tablet, or cell phone? (Circle any that apply.) How often?
- When or if you go online, what websites do you visit most?

- Do you play games? What kind of games do you play? (Board games, imagination games, video games, etc.)
- Name your favorite games:
- Do you have any hobbies? If so, what are they?
- If you had all the free time you wanted, what would you do with it?

- Any other interests, hobbies, likes or dislikes about what you do with your time outside of school? Or anything else I should know?

have had, how they tend to spend their free time, and what you can easily avoid and what you probably should learn more about.

You will likely want to go on a minor quest to immerse yourself in your students' cultural passions. But, unless you have several areas of interest, kids of your own around the same age, or lots of time on your hands, you likely will want to just pick one area to gain some expertise in. I tend to choose something different every year. My first year, I experimented with music. The next year it was television. Last year it was video games. Each year I have committed myself to learning about one aspect of pop culture, and I find myself floored by how much it has changed since I was a kid — or at least since I was younger. I ask kids what I should watch/listen/do. Then I jump in, looking for ways that understanding this world will in turn help me to better understand my students and impact my teaching.

Not so long ago I tried this with video games. When I was young, video games consisted of controllers and game cartridges. You could only play them plugged into your television set, by yourself, or maybe with one other player. Now, gamers can play games almost anywhere at any time. They can play on cell phones, tablets, dedicated portable devices, and consoles connected to the television. They can download the latest games. They can play with players beside them or halfway across the world. Many of these games require a level of problem solving and executive functioning, let alone vocabulary knowledge and memory, that is light-years ahead of the games of my own youth. I also learned by playing Minecraft, which was hugely popular at the time, how much learning happens when playing video games. It had been a long time since I had been in such a state of confusion and disequilibrium. I was reminded how frustrating and exhilarating it was to be a fresh learner at something. I carefully watched how the game taught me how to play while simultaneously keeping me from quitting.

One of the first and most immediate advantages that come from getting to know what's popular with students is getting to use it to help engage students. Very few things draw their eyes, hearts, and minds as quickly as pop cultural references. Even if they hate the reference at hand, it is still something that stirs the blood and helps kids sit up and pay attention. I have found that there are a variety of ways to do this:

- Open lessons with a pop culture reference or analogy. "You know, yesterday I was trying to play Mario Kart with my nephew," I might say. "There were things on the course, like the Mega Mushroom, that if I used them I could make things better for me, or other things like the banana peel that would make things worse for my opponents. That got me to thinking about our argumentative essays and how when we choose evidence we can think about how the evidence we choose either helps support our argument, or actually goes

into disproving our opponent's argument. The best essays, like the best Mario
Kart drivers, use a little bit of both."

- Use pop culture texts for practice texts.
  When I was working with the fifth-grade
  team at P.S. 63 in Manhattan, they were
  struggling to get their students invested in
  comparative literary essay. However, when
  we put away the short stories and articles
  and instead pulled out music, students were
  easily able to compare the themes with text
  details from Willow Smith's "Whip My Hair"
  and Katie Perry's "Fireworks." Once students
  saw what they could do with song lyrics they
  were able to transfer those skills to literature.
  (See Figure 12–2.)

- Use popular culture to teach tricky concepts
  like structure, craft, or meaning. When Pharell
  Williams' song "Happy" was all the rage, students were thrilled to take time to study the
  word choices, structural moves (repeated
  phrases, figurative language, purposeful use
  of pronouns), and even punctuation that
  helped pop out the meaning of the story.
  (See Figure 12–3.)

They then looked to see how they could apply that to
their own writing. When students were struggling
with balancing setting with action and dialogue, it
helped for them to see a clip of the show *Jessie* to see
that where the scene takes place, in a city taxi cab,
affects the actions and the dialogue.

By learning more about pop culture, I started to also see why
these things would be significant to my students. I understood the
camaraderie that comes from watching my team play basketball. I
saw the cultural cachet that comes from knowing all the lyrics to

When looking for themes in "Whip My Hair" we...
- Studied character actions
- Paid attention to setting
- Noticed lyrics
- Watched for char. change
- Listened for repeated lines
- Noted objects

When looking for themes in literature we can...
- Study character actions
- Pay attention to setting
- Notice dialogue
- Watch for char. change
- Mark repeated lines
- Note when objects are mentioned

Figure 12–2
Themes in Pop Songs

Persuasive Writing Moves We Can Learn from "Happy" by Pharell Williams
- Address audience → "You"
- Repeat position a lot!
- Can use comparisons, imagery and figurative language (fancy!)
- Chunk or group ideas into sections
- Use specific examples as evidence
- Leave out extra or distracting details
- Anticipate counter argument and then address it

Figure 12–3
Persuasive Writing in Pop Songs

the newest hit song. More and more I began to tap in to what made these things significant to my students. Most of what I discovered had to do with how these things made you feel, how they connected you with others, made you feel knowledgeable, allowed you to belong. Those were things I believed I could help kids dig into if they really wanted to write a research-based essay on the Brooklyn Nets. It's the humanity behind the culture that we can pull on.

I want to be clear: it is the humanity that I am after. In the name of doing what is best for kids, I will do whatever it takes. This may include studying what draws kids to pop culture and trying to bring a version of that to my teaching. For example, one of the things that makes video games such a powerful form of entertainment is that the player wants to return again and again. When researchers have studied why this is the case, they found one of the main reasons was the feedback that video games give to players and the environment they set up for play. When a player first starts a game they are given a small challenge, one that they might successfully complete, and get an immediate payoff of some sort (a coin, a new trick, an extra life). But if they do not succeed in the task, the game is built to give you gentle nudging in order to guide you to successfully complete the task. As the game progresses, the challenges get gradually harder, the rewards get bigger, and the risks for failure do as well. However, there is always immediate feedback, both positive and negative. This gradual support, with gradual growth in challenges and rewards, is exactly what we know works best for learning. If a student is dumped into a situation where the task is too challenging or they get feedback way after the fact, they become disheartened and are more likely to quit. I like to look at places in my teaching, like small-group work and conferences, where I can create an atmosphere of doable challenge and immediate feedback through guided practice or partner work.

That is just one example. Whenever we want to think of ways to draw our students closer to us, we can think—where do they spend the bulk of their spare time? How can I steal some of those tricks and apply it to my teaching? (See Figure 12–4.)

One caveat is worth mentioning—not all kids will know about or love pop culture. This is why it is so important to do that survey at the beginning of your year. If you have a class full of students who remain relatively unexposed to those things, you will likely want to leave it that way. This is not about converting students who are relatively unknowing about pop culture into aficionados, but rather another way to reach kids, for those of us who have a critical mass of students for whom this is the most important thing in their days.

Depending on how much of your classroom gets affected by pop culture, it will also be important for you to consider teaching some critical literacy skills. There are many sources for this work, especially Common Sense Media, which helps teachers guide students through understanding, questioning, and critiquing the media they are exposed to.

Figure 12–4 Some Ways to Use Pop Culture in the Classroom

Pop Culture Example	Ways It Can Be Used	How That Might Look/Sound
Music video with storyline *Examples: "What Does the Fox Say?" by Ylvis; "Wake Me Up" by Avecci*	• Study settings relationship to character and mood in narrative • Study character actions and motivations in narrative • Notice showing and not telling	"Writers, while you watch this video, I'd like you to pay close attention to how the setting is connected to the character's feeling and the mood of the story. As you watch, I'd also like you to be holding your own story in your mind and thinking about ways you could make those connections clearer."
Music video(s) with an idea *Examples: "Happy" by Pharrell Williams; "Whip My Hair" by Willow Smith*	• Identify the author's claim and how it is successfully communicated • Notice the reasons and supports the author gives • Notice the variety of evidence offered to support a claim (visual, lyrical, etc.) • Look for evidence of structure—how the video is broken into parts and organized	"Writers, as you watch this video, I want you to look to see if you can see the structure of a song and video you probably have heard before. When I was watching this video the other night, I almost felt like I could see the paragraphs that support the artist's claims. It made me think about the essay writing you have been doing lately."
Commercials or short films *Examples: Extra Gum-Origami Swan Ad, Cheerios Gracie Ad, Snack Attack Short film www.snackattackmovie.com*	• Look for how the story develops—in particular what is the character's motivation and how that affects the plot • The role of foreshadowing and the effect it has on readers/viewers • How the artist can show a theme through action and dialogue	"I am going to show you just the first half of this commercial. I want you to predict what you think will happen in the story. Then after we watch the second half, I want you to think about how the author planned the story so that it was surprising, but believable. Are there ways we can plan so that we can have the same effect on our readers?"
Video Games with Creation Powers: *Examples: Minecraft, Sims*	• Strategically planning • Using a variety of tools • Tapping experience from other similar games/writing experiences • Revising buildings so that they change and become different and better	"Writers, when I was playing Minecraft for the first time, I did not know what I was doing. I just wandered around in circles. And then I remembered from other games I've played that I should just touch everything I see. So I started to touch the trees. When I shook them I realized that was where the blocks came from. When we are writing, we too can lean on past experiences. We can think of other times we've written this type of genre and reuse those same skills."
Professional sports *Examples: Baseball, basketball, the Olympics*	• Perseverance in the face of difficulty • Planning • Building a variety of skills by studying other players (mentors) • Sharing work with other players (writers) in order to get feedback to improve	"When I was watching the World Series the other night, I noticed that the coaches were looking at papers and clearly had made a lot of plans for how to play the game. They wanted the story of the game to go a certain way, so they planned for it. As writers, we need to plan too. As much as we just want to rush in and play, we know our drafts and our final pieces will be better if we take the time to plan."

✳ Ongoing Work: When I Still Hate the Things My Kids Love

As I mentioned at the top of this chapter, I am the last person to be caught listening to Z100 or watching television for hours on end. I still am not a big consumer of pop culture. I do not think it is necessary for you, or me, or anyone who works with children, to think that their passions are amazing and wonderful. I don't know if this is strange or not, but when I don't like something I try to learn as much as I can about it. Many of the things that I am most knowledgeable about are things I actually don't like very much (cockroaches, rats, meat). However, I try to adapt an attitude of constant learning and growing. And every once in a while, in the act of studying something, I will find something I do like. But, in the meantime, know that by the simple act of not banning the things your kids hold nearest and dearest to their hearts, you are giving them a subtle but powerful message that their "real" lives need not be separated from their school lives. That, in fact, both lives will be the better for having merged.

13

Name Your Monster

If you've met me and talked to me for five minutes, you likely know I am a big Stephen King fan. This sometimes surprises people. "You don't strike me as a horror fan," they'll say. And the truth is, I am not a horror fan. I have tried a few other authors. And I have found some that I like. But in general I do not like horror. What I like about Stephen King is that most of his books start with a mysterious evil or bad thing that haunts or torments the characters in the story. Then, eventually, the mystery horror is named. Once that happens, the protagonist is better able to do battle with whatever that monster is. The other thing I love about Stephen King is that his characters are not those horror story tropes that go into dark rooms alone without a flashlight unable to scream. They do not cower in corners in fear. Instead, they are smart. They gather allies. They turn on lights. They gather weapons. They scream their heads off.

You have almost reached the end of this book. I'm hoping you've picked up some new ways to gather allies, turn on lights, gather weapons, and scream your heads off. And depending on how well I've done my job, you either have seen all of your major roadblocks to writing instruction addressed or you still have a few left. If you're a positive person, you're likely still hoping that I will manage to address it in the following pages. If you are a pessimist, you never thought I was going to address anything of value in the first place, and so you are completely unsurprised that yet another professional book has let you down. If you are a realist you know that there is no way any book could address all possible problems, but you are hoping that somehow the things you picked up from this book might help you. I imagine that all of you are at least partly correct.

It is true, there is no way that this or any book could address all of the possible issues and roadblocks that could come up in writing workshop. For every one that is addressed, there are three new ones developing. As I finished drafting this book, I heard several more questions from teachers that I wanted to address. But we are running out of time and pages. The good news is that I endeavor to address many of them on my blog, as a continuing conversation. And also, what I believe is more important, is that each of us develops our own framework or problem-solving strategy for whatever teaching issues come our way.

While I will say that over my years as an educator in various settings with wildly different needs and working with colleagues whose brilliance can make anyone's head spin has absolutely filled my coffers with strategies for dealing with a wide range of difficulties, it is also true that I regularly am faced, either in my own practice or while supporting another's practice, with a problem I don't have a ready solution for. In that case, I head for my tried-and-true strategies to help me attack the problem.

First off, let me say that I tend to believe there are problems that bother us and there are problems that don't. Some are simply annoying or time consuming, but they certainly don't keep us up at night. But the ones that do dig deep into our skin are often problems connected with our fears.

For example, as I mentioned earlier in the book, one of the comments I can't stand hearing from teachers is when a student is called lazy. I don't believe in lazy. As my writing teacher Jennifer Belle has repeated enough times it has become my mantra, "There is no such thing as lazy. Only fear." But I also could look at it from the other side — not just from the student's perspective. What is it about students who are behaving in ways that many teachers label lazy, that drives us absolutely nuts? I would argue that it too has a basis in fear. Let's list out the qualities and characteristics that get a student the label of "lazy":

- Often produces little or no work
- Doesn't seem to use tools provided very efficiently (word walls, charts, mentor texts, etc.)
- Physical posture is often slumping, spread out, or head down
- Seems bright but produced work doesn't match that perceived brightness

When looking at those characteristics listed out like that, I can imagine a few reasons that I, or another educator, might have some fears about working with him. I could imagine that I am afraid there are bigger issues happening at home that I have no way of fixing. Maybe there's a learning or attentional dysfunction of some sort that needs additional support and resources that I might not have access to. Perhaps the fear is that there is a way to reach him and we don't know what the secret is. As I start to name out these fears one by one, I can say that most of them fit under the umbrella that I am afraid I cannot help him, so I am unconsciously passing the buck over to the child's shoulders by labeling him lazy. Rather than do that, I should probably seek input from other professionals to address as many of his struggles as I can reasonably do.

I find that if I am triggered by something, if a problem burrows into my skin, I am likely afraid of some aspect of it. It helps me a lot to name out the characteristics of the situation, just like we did above with the child being labeled lazy. Often in the naming of the characteristics I am able to see what I am actually afraid of. Here's a nonschool true example. I was afraid of flying for a long time. Like, taking-prescribed-drugs-to-get-on-a-flight afraid. The more I flew, the more it became a problem. So I decided to take a fear-of-flying course. As part of it, the instructor (a pilot) asked us to list out our actual concerns. I just kept saying— "I'm afraid of flying!," but he responded with, "But what *about* flying are you afraid of?" So, despite my sweaty palms I listed all the things I was actually afraid of under that heading, as embarrassing as they were:

- The plane running out of fuel so the plane crashes
- Losing an engine so the plane crashes
- The wall of the airplane peeling away and me getting sucked out of the plane
- The plane losing oxygen so I suffocate

When I looked at the list I had a nice list of fears. But I also saw that I could get information and grapple with each of them one at a time. Like, for example, I learned plane crashes are incredibly unlikely, but in the event that one happened, you have more than a 50 percent chance of surviving! And I also learned that planes coming apart and you getting sucked out of the plane was even rarer. But more importantly, when I looked across all my fears, I realized that they pointed to one overarching fear—fear of not being in control. Once I realized that was what it was, it made a lot more sense why my instructor kept saying "Flying is always a choice." Every time I fly I am choosing to do so. So I actually am in control and choosing to hand it over to someone else. Believe it or not, that simple exercise of naming out my biggest fears, looking for a pattern, naming it, and then thinking how I could act in the face of that fear helped me vanquish it. Whenever I get on a plane (at least once a month) and I feel that little tickle of fear, I remind myself: I am choosing to be on this plane. I am choosing to be on this plane because there is somewhere I want to go, something I want to do. It is worth it to me to overcome my fear, and take any risks that might be there, because I want to be where this plane is taking me.

I would also argue that the same is true for most problems we are having in our writing classrooms. We can point to a problem. Usually we name the problem as something out there. But if we start to list the characteristics about it—what bothers us about it, we often realize something more. Sometimes that something more leads us to a solution. Sometimes it leads us to a greater understanding that can help us to achieve a sort of acceptance. You might try this right now. Grab a writing utensil.

1. Name a problem in your writing workshop:

2. How do you know it's a problem? You might start by listing out the characteristics of that problem. This can be just things that are pieces of the problem, a list of things you don't like about it, or just a line-by-line description of it. This could be some of the bad effects you've experienced or witnessed. Try to aim for two or more descriptors.

3. Where do you feel stuck? Now look across your jots so far. What pattern are you seeing? What is the thing that is holding you back that you don't naturally just have a solution for? Is it a fear? Is it an inability to think of a solution?

4. Rename your problem or fear as a realization or goal. This is where things get dirty. And, even if you are truly an optimist you will need to skate over to pessimist land for a bit. And you pessimists out there—you will need to borrow a cup of sugar from your optimist neighbor. The best way to do this step is to think of both sides of the coin.

This last step might require that you face some things you don't like to look at. Some of the monsters that exist in our teaching lives are very real. There are children who are abused and neglected. There are corrupt politicians who pass laws that directly affect your classroom. There are teacher evaluations that take none of what matters most into account. And those are just things that exist in the education realm. There are also universal human truths that just seep through our classroom walls. Issues of jealousy and insecurity and the knowledge that there is a very real chance that we won't be able to help every student we want to help. That not everything that comes into our purview is under our control, or even our responsibility. Looking at these things will hopefully help you to see what you can and cannot actually do something about. No, you won't be able to eradicate child poverty. But you might be able to create a goal of making sure that the students in your class who need food get nourishment on a more regular basis. No, you might not be able to fix the fact that your primary service provider for your students with IEPs does not see eye to eye with you on writing workshop. But you could make a goal of trying to arrange the students' schedules so as to minimize the interruptions in their writing time.

One way to do this is to try to use what patterns you saw when looking across your list. What does this pattern say about you? What does it say about your situation? See if you can rename your monster as a challenge that you can overcome. "Intimidated by new state writing standards" can become "Need to revise curriculum so that it is both philosophically and standards aligned." "Teacher evaluations make me feel like my writing curriculum needs to be more traditional and make me scared to teach workshop" could be renamed as, "I need to get clearer on what and why I am teaching writing the way I do and then learn to articulate it better."

Simply naming a problem, after identifying it as a fear or not, is not always going to be enough to make things better. So, in that case, you might consider making a plan of action. You might refer to the various plans offered in this book as a template, you might devise your own plan, or you might decide to seek advice from other sources. But, no matter what you decide to do, while setting your plan up and thinking of your objectives and actions, you might want to bear in mind Gabriel Oettingen's work. We are all more likely to vanquish more of our monsters if we not only envision our plan and the monster's demise, but also if we anticipate the obstacles we will face and make a plan for overcoming those as well.

So let's try this whole process with a problem I often hear (and have shared with others myself): "Writing workshop is not working. My kids are not writing like they should be." You might decide to pick another problem and try that one out instead. (See Figure 13–1.)

Of course, I don't think there's anything magical about working through a problem this way. It's a combination of many different problem-solving protocols. And certainly not even every step needs to be taken. Sometimes, just naming the monster that is your problem is enough, much like turning on the lights when you were a kid let you see that the monster in the corner of your bedroom was just a pile of dirty laundry. I also think that for some

Figure 13–1 Name the Problem

Name the problem:	"Writing workshop is not working. My kids are not writing like they should be."
How do you know it's a problem?	• Several of my students do not write during workshop time. • The students who do write are only writing versions of what I have modeled. • I spend a long time planning lessons that are not used by the students. • When I confer I mostly work to make sure every student understands the lesson.
Where do you feel stuck?	I am doing more work than my students are.
What are you most afraid will happen?	I desperately want my students to do well with writing workshop and am afraid that they won't.
Rename the fear as a realization or goal:	I need to build my students' writing independence.
Name the roadblocks that might get in the way:	• Student work won't be of as high a quality as I would like. • Students won't try everything I teach. • My administrator might wonder why I am letting my students do things that are different than what I am teaching.
How might you deal with those roadblocks:	• Expect that some finished work might not be as high quality, but the process will likely be stronger. Revise rubric to reflect those things. • Point out students who try things taught in class, as well as students who develop their own strategies. Elevate the use of a variety of strategies rather than particular strategies. • Have a conversation with my principal about my goal of more independence. Align it with my other professional goals. Let her know that I expect messiness, but hope she will bear with me.
Plan	• Introduce independent writing projects. • Make sure my unit-based lessons are short and offer choice. • Involve students more in chart and other tool making. • Encourage interdependence across partnerships.

people, making a struggle public is enough. It's the secretive nature of having a struggle that can cause the stress.

Still others will find that turning a negative into a positive, or seeing the good side of the problem, will be the way to address their concerns. So instead of saying, "I don't know enough," that teacher might say, "I will learn more." This can be a very valid stance to take, especially if you are a naturally optimistic person. By positing the issue as a directive to action, you are already well on the way to improving the situation.

Ultimately, if I were to say what I think is the most important thing I hope readers of this book take away, I would say it is this: Naming your monster is important. By naming your monster you are already well on your way to becoming proactive in your problem solving. Just as there is power in the Stephen King protagonist naming the monster in the first place, there is even greater power in later giving that monster a new name — a name that lessens its hold over you and also gives you a battle plan.

But most important, *by far*, is that when faced with something that tries to stop us from doing what we know is good for kids, we as educators owe it to ourselves and our students to take action. We are deciding it is worth it to face our fears and get on the scary plane that is called teaching. Where we are going, where we want our students to go, is worth it. We don't just complain about it and stay on the ground. We don't wait for someone else to come along to get on the plane for us. We might not know the perfect answer. But we can try something. We can ask for help. We can make motions toward making things better. Because as long as we try to make change, as long as we actively try to be open to making things better, we will be unstoppable.

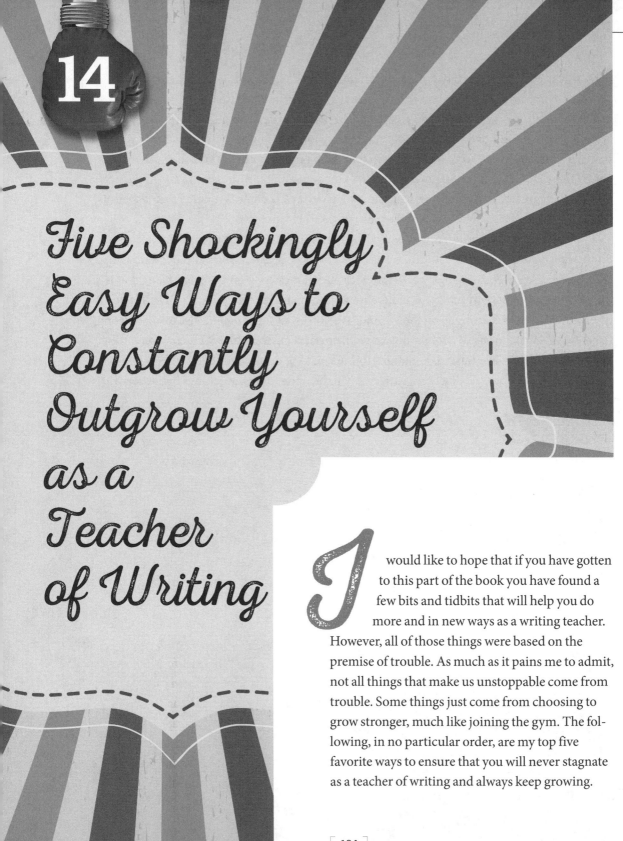

14

Five Shockingly Easy Ways to Constantly Outgrow Yourself as a Teacher of Writing

I would like to hope that if you have gotten to this part of the book you have found a few bits and tidbits that will help you do more and in new ways as a writing teacher. However, all of those things were based on the premise of trouble. As much as it pains me to admit, not all things that make us unstoppable come from trouble. Some things just come from choosing to grow stronger, much like joining the gym. The following, in no particular order, are my top five favorite ways to ensure that you will never stagnate as a teacher of writing and always keep growing.

1. *Write.* There is nothing more important for a writing teacher to do than to write. Around the writing workshop community, you will often hear teachers say, "You wouldn't take dance classes from someone who didn't dance. Why would you expect kids to learn to write from someone who doesn't write?" And while there is truth in that, I feel like the real reasons teachers should write are far more complex.

   One of the main reasons I think writing teachers need to write is that it helps keep us grounded. Never am I more patient or kind than when I am working on a writing project. I know what it feels like to write a sentence and then immediately hate it. I know what it feels like to want to do anything in the world, including clean the bathroom, rather than write. When we write often we are reminded of just how hard a task it is.

   Another reason I think it is so crucial that we write is that our students need to have models. While they might see people reading every day, the chances are good that they rarely see the adults in their lives writing for any length of time. Watching us write, reading our work, hearing our stories about our struggles, helps bring writing out of the realm of magic and into reality.

   I do want to say one thing that might differ from other advice you have read about regularly writing. I have read and heard from many, many writers and teachers of writing that you need to write every day. I don't agree with that. I have managed to write several books mostly writing one evening a week. And quite frankly, that evening can range in time from ten minutes to five hours. It just depends on how much time I have, where I am in a project, and if there are any children teething or vomiting (not students, my offspring). While I don't believe that you need to write every day, or even for very long, I do think that making writing a regular practice (fifteen minutes after school on Mondays) will make it more likely that you get the most benefit from it. It's the regularity and predictability of it that makes it work. You live and think differently when you know your writing time is coming up.

   Another key benefit of writing regularly is that I am rarely at a loss for what to teach my students. Every time I hit upon a struggle or find a writing success in my personal writing, I have also gathered a new strategy I can teach to students. When I write I virtually guarantee I will have an endless supply of teaching points.

   You might be wondering, what can I write? You can start by just trying the lessons you will be teaching to your students. Or maybe you can write that editorial about how hard-working teachers are for your local paper. Maybe you can get going on the novel you have wanted to write since college. Perhaps you want to write a blog or professional book for other teachers. It doesn't matter what you write, as long as you are writing.

As a way to support your individual writing work, you might want to consider joining a writing group — or writing workshop for adults. Writing in the company of others, or at least sharing our writing with other writers, is a helpful and humbling experience. I have been a member of writing groups for over two decades. I owe my continued efforts as a writer to the fact that I have a community that I must share my writing with, who knows my writing quirks and strengths, and gives me another layer of accountability.

If you are wondering how you can find a writing group, there are a few possibilities. The easiest one is to just hang a sign in the teacher's lounge inviting any colleagues who'd like to join you. In one school I know, the teachers meet once a month at the local bar to write and share their writing. But an empty classroom would also suffice. You could consider going to a university or looking in writing trade magazines like *Poets & Writers* for mentions of writing groups. Many bookstores and libraries also host regular writing groups. If you are fortunate to be in a community where there are many different writing groups available, you might consider choosing your group based on who is leading it. Ideally your group will be led by a writer, preferably a published writer. It would be better still if you have read and admired that writer's work. My longest-running writing teacher, Jennifer Belle, was a novelist whose work I admired before I joined her writing group.

Once you have a writing group you attend, you will want to get as many teaching advantages from it as possible. One of the biggest gifts I got from writing groups, aside from accountability, is learning how to make laser-sharp comments and critiques. While I tend to speak with more gentleness with children, I do find that the practice of regularly reading other people's works in progress has made it easier for me to spot teaching points on the fly.

Another great side benefit is that often, receiving critique regularly helps make us understand how nerve-wracking it can be to share writing with others — something our students do daily.

2. *Mirror write on a regular basis.* When I think of one of the most powerful
   tools I started to use later in my teaching career, one that I consistently learn
   from and am surprised by, I point to mirror writing.

   Demonstration writing is important. We have been taught this by all the
   greats: Donald Graves, Donald Murray, Lucy Calkins, Carl Anderson, Georgia
   Heard—the list goes on. However, demonstration writing alone can sometimes not be enough. Sometimes we write too high for our students to follow
   what we are modeling. Sometimes we are too simplistic in our efforts to make
   our models more accessible. We also sometimes tuck in way too much to
   teach in any one demonstration. When I discovered mirror writing I realized
   that all of those troubles were solved in one fell swoop.

   The way mirror writing typically goes is that teachers choose a piece of student writing that is typical of many students in her class. She then spends
   some time reading the piece very closely and looking for what the student *is*
   doing as a writer. Not looking at what
   is absent. Looking at what is present.
   There's a reason for this. We can't mirror something that is not there, only
   what *is* there. Then, the teacher usually thinks of a topic she can write
   about that is different, but can hit
   the same points the student piece
   hits. For example, in the piece in
   Figure 14–1 the student is writing a
   narrative scene. There are characters speaking to each other and
   there is tension. So, I might decide
   to write a scene about two girls
   walking home from school and
   one friend is trying to convince
   the other friend to run for school
   council.

   The next piece in Figure 14–2
   is to actually try to mirror what
   the writer did, as close as possible to the moves they made. It

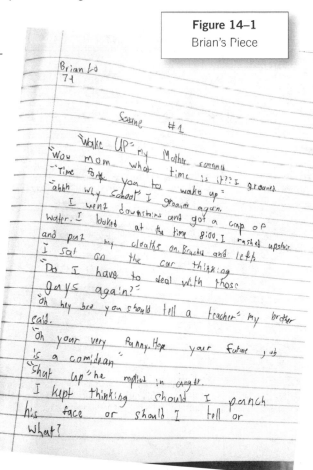

Figure 14–1
Brian's Piece

Figure 14–2
Finished Mirror Piece

helps a lot to name what the writer did first, as you are mirroring, so that you can be sure you are on the same pace, doing the same moves. So, for Brian's piece, I might list out for the first half:

Draft

"Come on " Stacia called.
"I'm coming as fast as I can," I complained.
"You can go faster"
"geez I'm coming" I complained again.
I got my backpack and headed toward our meeting spot. I walked to the corner. I went as fast as I could and waved to her as I came. Stood and smiled. I started walking besides her.
"Did you see those signs about student council?"
"Yeah I did I think you should run" Stacia said.
"No way. You're the one who's going to be president by the time you're 18."
"Not a chance" She answered in a laugh. I was wondering if maybe I should run with Stacia or maybe not at all?

- Starts with dialogue and simple dialogue tag

- Another piece of dialogue, a question, with tag

- Another piece of dialogue without tag

- Another piece of dialogue, with an exclamation, with a tag

- Four sentences of action

Then, my mirroring might look like this:

Student writes	I mirror
"Wake UP" my Mother screamed.	"Come on" Stacia called.
"Wow mom what time is it?" I groaned.	"I'm coming as fast as I can," I complained.
"Time for you to wake up."	"You can go faster."
"ahhh why school" I groaned again.	"geeez I'm coming" I complained again.
I went downstairs and got a cup of water. I looked at the time 8:00. I rushed upstairs and put my clothes on. Brushed and left. I sat on the car thinking.	I got my backpack and headed toward our meeting spot. I walked to the corner. I went as fast as I could and waved to her as I came. Stood and smiled. I started walking beside her.

By the end of mirror writing a kid's piece, a few incredibly helpful things happen. First and foremost, you now have a perfectly tailored piece of writing to demonstrate with, that encapsulates lots of teaching points you can use with students without writing above or below their ability level. You can also pick an assortment of pieces from different levels or with different patterns so that you have a repertoire of pieces to turn to in order to highlight certain strategies to teach. But also handy is how much we learn about the young writer when we endeavor to write exactly like him. We can see how those sentence constructions happen. We can better theorize why they decided right then to add a fancy vocabulary word or to add some dialogue. We have an insider's view. Some teachers I have worked with who use this method report that when mirror writing they feel more empathetic to the student, as well as more positive. It is not looking from a deficit model (since you can't write what is not there), so there is much more to see and appreciate. I have come to believe that mirror writing is not only a powerful tool to use over and over again for actual instruction, because the teaching ideas will be endless, but also a very powerful tool to stay grounded with students' current and real abilities, and not perceived ones.

3. *Read books written for professional writers.* Many teachers of writing read books written for teachers — such as this one. And these books are important (thank you for reading!). However, while you're at it, I believe it will behoove you to also read books written by professional authors for professional writers. These are books that are purely about the writing. They discuss craft, structure, even history of a genre. They are jam-packed with writing tips and ideas. Not all of them will be appropriate for children. But enough of them will be, that it will be worth your while.

   I suggest that you start off first with more general writing books such as one of my favorites, *On Writing* by Stephen King, or *Writing Tools* by Roy Peter Clark, or *On Writing* by Eudora Welty. From there you might want to make forays into books that are about particular styles, types, or concerns you want to learn more about. Many of these books have extensive bibliographies that can in turn help you find more books to read.

   As with almost all of my suggestions in this chapter, it matters less what you read, than that you do just take the time to read. It's the act of actively learning about the craft of writing, and not just about the teaching of writing, that will feed your practice in rich and transformative ways.

4. *Read lots of examples of the sorts of texts you want students to write.* This should include examples for children as well as for adults. When I was looking to teach students how to write fantasy stories, I was tempted to stick only to children's fantasy since my students would only be writing on a children's level. However, I knew that the more examples of a genre I had under my belt the better, so I ventured over into books written for adults as well. Once I switched over to adult fantasy, I saw some new aspects of the genre, at the children's level (such as tricky vocabulary and long, descriptive passages), that I had missed because the children's and young adult books weren't a challenge for me as a reader. By the end of reading a pile of adult examples of a genre, I had a very strong sense of what was crucial to include and teach in the genre, as well as what could be tweaked or left out.

Of course, reading lots of examples of children's texts will give lots of other payoffs as well. You will be better positioned to build libraries for mentor texts, for example. You can also make a point of reading with sticky notes in hand to mark up any writing moves you notice that you could later turn into teaching points for whole-class, small-group, or one-on-one instruction.

Additionally, by reading lots of examples of the types of texts you want your students to write, you will begin to develop a felt sense of what you are hoping for them to achieve.

5. *Put you and your life outside of school first.* When I first considered being an educator, one of the things I imagined, and rather liked about it, was the idea that being a teacher was one of those jobs a person could get completely lost in — you will always be needed. There's always a student who needs more, a curriculum that needs to be written, papers that need to be graded, a room that needs to be straightened. I loved the romance of the heroic overworked teacher who would never have enough time to do all that she needed to do, but still carried on.

Then I got my first classroom.

And I stayed every day at school until at least 7:00 pm. And brought work home. And worked all weekend long. I never stopped working. My parents worried about me. My romantic life collapsed. My friends barely spoke to me. And on the last day of school, after I ushered my class out the door and into their summer vacations, I returned to my empty classroom and faced the piles of work that was never graded, the data that was never analyzed, and still more piles of curriculum that never got taught. I dumped it all into the garbage. All of it. As far as I know, it never really mattered that I didn't get to all of it. In that moment, as I stood over the three overflowing trashcans, I truly realized that teaching as a profession is a bottomless pit. It will never be finished. It will never be enough.

So instead of getting on the hopeless hamster wheel of expending all of my energy and still ending up nowhere, I adopted that philosophy you might remember from Chapter 1 — *work smarter not harder*. That simple overused expression has become my mantra.

I have taken it to mean, to me anyway, that whenever I sit down to work I need to ask myself, "Do I need or want to do this?" If the answer is yes I go on to ask myself, "Is this the best possible way I can work in order to get this job done?" If there are more efficient ways to work — such as asking someone for advice, or working with colleagues — I'll change tacks and try some other way. If there are no better ways to work, I can be satisfied knowing that I am working smarter. When I work this way I can actually get more of the important things that need to get done completed. It also gives me a deep satisfaction to tick things off my to-do list. Additionally, making a conscious effort to not spin my wheels to work on something that is not that important, or could be finished more efficiently, gives me more of something that we all know we never have enough of: time.

What does a teacher do with extra time? As we've established, there are countless things we can do with that time. We can create new bulletin boards, write curriculum, read student work, study data, plan for small groups, read professional literature . . . the list is endless. But we could also do something that I am a huge advocate for: take some time for yourself.

I can already see some of you shaking your heads. I know, the idea of a teacher taking actual time for him or herself *during the school year* is just an off-the-hook notion. But hear me out. I think it is one of the single most important things an excellent teacher who plans to be an educator for the long haul needs to do. And as a fellow educator and a parent of two, I have a vested interest in dedicated educators staying in the field for the long haul.

Research tells us there are things that make a huge impact on how people perform. One of those things is the amount of sleep we get. Another is how happy we are. When we are overstressed and unhappy we simply cannot perform at the same levels we would if we were well rested with a smile on our faces. But this would be true no matter what job you were performing. As a teacher of writing you owe yourself a special debt—and perhaps just as importantly your students—to take care of yourself.

For one thing, when you spend time away from the classroom and away from work you are doing things you can share with your students and use for your own writing. Whether it's sitting on a bench watching birds or going to a friend's birthday party, those are life experiences that are worthy of being present for and also worth writing about. We also feel more real, less robo-teacher, when students know we have lives outside of school. We are already high on a pedestal in many of their minds, but when we share our everyday life foibles, frustrations, and joys, they can see that we are in fact real people with lives outside of school and our opinions can count more.

Additionally, when we have rich lives outside of the classroom we are more empathetic to people who also have things to do, and we are more likely to come up with strategies to help them get a better balance. When all we do is work and occasionally eat and sleep, it is hard for us to help the student who is trying to balance his love of baseball with his writing life. After all, we aren't really trying to balance anything ourselves.

But when David shows up with his empty notebook again, and he confesses that it's because of playoff season, instead of taking away recess, we can pull up a chair and have a heart-to-heart. "Oh, you feel too busy to write? I get that," we can say to David. "I know I feel that way with my knitting and seeing my friends and spending time with my family. But you know what I do? I just take some time first thing in the morning, before I even get out of bed, to do some writing. That way all the events of the day before are still fresh, and I haven't really gotten lost in the new day's events." Or insert whatever strategy you actually use to get work done without interrupting your life.

I would say that the first step in making our lives a bigger priority is to actually make a commitment to doing it. If you do not feel that spending less time working and more time doing things outside and away from school is a worthwhile endeavor, then none of the tips I can give you will work. However, if you have decided (or someone in your life has decided for you) that you need more of a balance, there are a few things you can try.

One thing I found helpful when I was reaching toward balance was to sign up for a class or writing group that meets on a weekly basis, preferably close-ish to dismissal time so that you need to pack up your bag and leave earlier at least one day a week. My ideal activity is one that I've paid for. I came to this after I started my own writing group with a few friends in my living room, and with no financial commitment, and very forgiving friends, it was all too easy for me to cancel it for schoolwork. If that sounds like too big of a plan for you, another winning option is to become the person in your grade who is responsible for getting all the other teachers out to the local coffee shop, or bar, for a Friday social. When you are in charge, it is next to impossible to be the one who lags behind to finish just "one more thing."

One wise teacher I know bought a smaller school bag in the effort to hold back the tide. She said that anything that did not fit into her bag would have to stay at school or come home another day. This requires a fair amount of self-control, and also only works if your school is not tech-heavy. If you are dealing with a tech-savvy school where you could access almost anything you needed to work away from the building, I suggest you set up a timer to cut yourself off after a certain time. Let's say 8:00 on weeknights and 7:00 on weekends, to start. This could involve simply an alarm telling you to stop working. For those of us who are workaholics, you can program your computer or gadget to power down at that time. I personally opt for the lower-tech options. I always sit with my family during dinner (even if I have plans to eat something different later) and stay with them through bedtime. If I have to pull out a gadget or piece of work in their time with me, I announce a strict time limit. "I have to send one email. I will only be using this for ten minutes." My older son is better than any alarm clock, as he starts to pull on my arm. "It's been ten minutes, Mommy. Work is closed. It's playtime."

My partner and I have a monthly set date night, where we have a babysitter already booked—which means if we cancel we still have to pay her. While we can of course have additional nights out, the set monthly date night guarantees that we will at least have that one night just for fun (as opposed to a school meeting or a familial obligation). I also like to double-down and try to buy tickets for a concert, play, or lecture a long time before the event, even if I don't have to, because for some reason tickets to something feel like a bigger commitment than almost anything else.

No matter how you do it, when first reaching for a work/life balance, one of the earliest steps you'll need to make is to carve out regular and noncancelable time just for you.

For those of you who are still unconvinced, and even the thought of spending time on something other than work makes you break out in a guilty rash, please try to remember that your students will actually be better served from a well-rounded, rested, happier teacher—even if that means the papers won't be graded as quickly and the bulletin boards aren't all Pinterest worthy. After all, in our striving for perfection we actually find ourselves more often than not keeping ourselves from finishing or appreciating the very work we are so dedicated to. When I heard that Sheryl Sandberg of *Lean In* fame had a sign in her office that read, "Done is better than perfect," I realized I had a new mantra to add to my collection.

Final Thoughts:
An Honor Flight

Tighten those laces and march toward the battlefield.

Meet it head on, that is exactly what firefighters, doctors, and teachers do too— every day.

Lately I have been thinking a lot about how hard it is to be a teacher right now. Perhaps the hardest it's ever been. And I started to think of other hard times in history. I kept coming back to the image of the soldier that Barb's husband is, and how he often exhorted his educator wife to "tighten those laces and head to the battlefield."

It all brought to mind the patriarch of my family, my Uncle Louis. He's a ninety-one-year-old World War II veteran. He enlisted in the Marines right after Pearl Harbor. He was with the Marines 2nd Division. One hundred eighty highly trained, very effective soldiers in his division, who didn't lose a soldier until Okinawa.

My uncle's last battle was in Okinawa. The bloodiest battle in the South Pacific theatre. He lost his leg when a bomb landed in the ditch he and his fellow soldiers were holed up in. The guy next to him made a tourniquet for my uncle's leg with his belt, and lost his pants in the process. My uncle remembered laughing and then passed out.

When my uncle woke up in the military hospital, he found out that he was losing his leg and that out of the 180 soldiers he was with, only six had survived. The soldier who had saved my uncle's life with his belt wasn't one of the six.

My uncle went on to marry, raise five children, run a successful beauty salon, and sing chorus in the San Diego Opera. He has lived a full life. About two years ago I got word that he had been invited to go on an Honor Flight. Do you know what an honor flight is? If you don't know what it is, you might consider watching a trailer for a documentary about the program. It is worth the few minutes it will take to watch it. Trust me. www.youtube.com/watch?v=9E7GLdYhm3s

For those who don't know, it's an organization that pays for World War II veterans to travel, all expenses paid, to Washington, DC to see their memorial. The one that took sixty-five years to be built. Now, because so many of the veterans are dying, it's a race against time.

My partner, my older son, and I met my dad and Uncle Louis at the memorial. We toured all the great DC sites. My uncle was stoic through it all. A dapper man wearing a blazer and carrying a cane, he eventually tired and needed to sit in a wheelchair, which my father and I took turns pushing the rest of the day.

It was truly an incredible sight to see these gentlemen pile out of the bus after it pulled up to the memorial, met by honor guards and waving crowds. As we waited for my uncle to emerge from the bus, we stood behind some bikers wearing Vietnam Vet leather jackets, applauding and cheering. I heard one of them say, as an old man in a walker shuffled by, his military cap nested on his silver hair, "These guys are the real deal. There is no one tougher than these guys."

Toward the end of the monument tour, I asked my uncle if there was anything he definitely wanted to see before the buses moved on to Arlington National Cemetery. He said he wanted to see the Lincoln Memorial. We raced toward it, my dad hobbling along with a cane, my partner pushing a stroller, me pushing my uncle's wheelchair. When we got up to the statue, somehow my Uncle and I got separated from our group. But, since we only had minutes to spare, I raced him over to Lincoln. I stood behind my uncle and watched as his head turned upward. Then I felt his hand grab mine. He placed it against his cheek. I felt wetness. I heard his voice rasp, "Do you feel that?"

"Yes," I said.

"That's the first tear I shed for that war. I just couldn't do it. I could not do it. It was a hell of a thing. I was blown to bits. But I lived. They didn't. And they were the better men."

I stayed silent. I didn't know what to say.

"They deserved to be here. I don't. But I am still so grateful that I am here."

My uncle was one of those soldiers who tightened his bootlaces and headed straight toward the battlefield.

Here's the thing though. I believe you are too. I believe that all teachers are. We didn't get into this business to sit around with kids who already knew everything, who could already do everything. We got into this business because we wanted to teach. We wanted to make students fall in love with learning. We wanted to help students learn how to tell their life stories, to craft them in a way that no one could ignore. We became teachers because we wanted to head into that big messy business of education where we don't get to choose our students or our standards *or even our furniture*. We chose this big messy battlefield of education because we wanted to make a difference in the life of a child.

In the introduction of this book, I asked you to consider yourself akin to firefighters, doctors, soldiers, like my uncle the World War II soldier—who, when they hear of trouble, don't turn and run away like any sane individual would do. But rather, they tighten their laces and march toward where the trouble is.

Throughout this book I have presented troubles teachers have shared with me throughout my years as an educator, from their classrooms, in workshops, via letters, and through social media. I have done my best to offer you the wisest tips, suggestions, and strategies I know for the problems I have heard the most. Some of them will work. Some of them won't. Some of your biggest troubles won't even have been mentioned in this book. But I want you to know that it doesn't really matter. That going through this book, whether just skimming the chapters you wanted to read or in a study group or with a partner, was important work. What you did there, in your mind, with your colleagues, envisioning the battlefield, planning for it, was just a dress rehearsal of what you'll do countless times throughout this school year and the next. You, like so many educators before you, and so many who will come after you, are knowingly signing up yet again for another year of joy and laughter, frustration and disappointment, amazing stories and growth, tears and countless battlefields to march into.

And just like those young people from seventy years ago enlisted to the service of our country, knowing the dangers, expecting the risks, but believing the conflict in front of them was too important to turn away from, you too have volunteered for service of another kind. It's a different sort of battlefield, with different sorts of conflicts to face. But it is fraught with struggle, problems, and a distinct advantage in having just a little bit of a pessimistic streak so that you aren't caught unawares.

In a quiet moment after the Lincoln Memorial, I asked my Uncle Louis if he ever regretted going to war, or enlisting in the Marines. He had lost his friends, his fiancée, his livelihood, his leg.

He said, never once. He knew where he was needed. He tightened his laces and went. His only regret was that *he didn't do more*.

Then he turned to me and said, in his raspy voice, "But, teachers, ah, are heroes too. Teachers are the ones that make sure this all"—he gestured to the grand monuments around us—"keeps rolling along."

And that got me thinking . . .

If I was in charge of the universe, I would make it that there was a memorial for teachers built in Washington, DC. One that honored all that you do and all those who came before you did. All the battles waged, some lost, many won. All the lives saved as we were up to our necks in the muck of it all.

And I would send you on an honor flight. I wouldn't wait until sixty-five years from now. I would do it very soon. I would do it every year in perpetuity. Teachers would receive all-expense-paid trips to their nation's capital to view their very own monument. You would be greeted at the airport by a choir of singers, a marching band, flags, and an *honor guard of students*, past and present, holding handmade signs, waving pom poms and tossing flowers, thanking you for all you have done, for all those you have taught to love learning, to discover their own story, to hone their craft so that their writing is worthy of their hearts. I would send you on an Honor Flight to thank you for all that you have done and continue to do as you gear up for the battlefields that still need to be marched toward.